# GROUPS

the
life-giving
power of
community

# GROUPS

## the life-giving power of community

JOHN ORTBERG,
LAURIE PEDERSON,
JUDSON POLING

PURSUING SPIRITUAL TRANSFORMATION

ZONDERVAN™

GRAND RAPIDS, MICHIGAN 49530

WILLOW
CREEK
RESOURCES

We want to hear from you. Please send your comments about this book to us in care of the address below. Thank you.

## ZONDERVAN™

GRAND RAPIDS, MICHIGAN 49530

w w w . z o n d e r v a n . c o m

## ZONDERVAN™

*Groups: The Life-Giving Power of Community*
Copyright © 2000 by the Willow Creek Association

Requests for information should be addressed to:

Zondervan, *Grand Rapids, Michigan 49530*

ISBN 0-310-22076-9

All Scripture quotations unless otherwise noted are taken from the *Holy Bible: New International Version*®. NIV®. Copyright © 1973, 1978, 1984 by International Bible Society. Used by permission of Zondervan. All rights reserved.

We are grateful for permission given by a number of gifted teachers to use excerpts from their books and messages for the opening readings in the sessions. These authors and speakers are acknowledged throughout this guide.

*Interior design by Laura Klynstra Blost*

*Printed in the United States of America*

02 03 04 05 /❖ EP/ 10 9 8 7 6

# CONTENTS

# *Pursuing Spiritual Transformation*

The Pursuing Spiritual Transformation series is all about being spiritual. But that may not mean what you think!

Do you consider yourself a spiritual person? What does that mean? Does spiritual growth seem like an impossible amount of work? Do you have a clear picture of the kind of life you'd live if you were to be more spiritual?

Each guide in the Pursuing Spiritual Transformation series is dedicated to one thing — helping you pursue authentic spiritual transformation. Here, the focus is growing through relationships.

You may find this study different from others you have done in the past. Each week in preparation for your group meeting, you will be completing a Bible study and experimenting with a variety of spiritual exercises. These elements are designed to enhance your private times with God and, in turn, to help you invite him into all aspects of your life, even the everyday routines. After all, spiritual life is just *life*—the one you live moment by moment.

It is very important that you complete this work before going to each meeting because the discussion is based on what you've learned from the study and what you've observed as a result of the spiritual exercise. The Bible study and exercises are not meant to be done an hour before the meeting, quickly filling in the blanks. Instead, we suggest you thoughtfully and prayerfully complete them over the course of several days as part of your regular devotional time with God.

A good modern Bible translation, such as the New International Version, the New American Standard Bible, or the New Revised Standard Version, will give you the most help in your study. You might also consider keeping a Bible dictionary handy to look up unfamiliar words, names, or places. Write your responses in the spaces provided in the study guide or use your personal journal if you need more space. This will help you participate more fully in the discussion, and will also help you personalize what you are learning.

When your group meets, be willing to join in the discussion. The leader of the group will not be lecturing but will encourage people to discuss what they have learned from the study and exercise. Plan to share what God has taught you. Try to be sensitive to the other members of the group. Listen attentively when they speak, and be affirming whenever you can. This will encourage more hesitant members of the group to participate. Be careful not to dominate the discussion. By all means participate, but allow others to have equal time. If you are a group leader or a participant who wants further insights, you will find additional comments in the Leader's Guide at the back of the study.

We believe that your ongoing journey through this material will place you on an exciting path of spiritual adventure. Through your individual study time and group discussions, we trust you will enter into a fresh concept of spiritual life that will delight the heart of God . . . and your heart too!

# Ten Core Values
# for Spiritual Formation

Spiritual transformation . . .

> . . . is essential, not optional, for Christ-followers.

> . . . is a process, not an event.

> . . . is God's work, but requires my participation.

> . . . involves those practices, experiences, and relationships that help me live intimately with Christ and walk as if he were in my place.

> . . . is not a compartmentalized pursuit. God is not interested in my spiritual life; he's interested in my *life*—all of it.

> . . . can happen in every moment. It is not restricted to certain times or practices.

> . . . is not individualistic, but takes place in community and finds expression in serving others.

> . . . is not impeded by a person's background, temperament, life situation, or season of life. It is available right now to all who desire it.

> . . . and the means of pursuing it, will vary from one individual to another. Fully devoted followers are handcrafted, not mass-produced.

> . . . is ultimately gauged by an increased capacity to love God and people. Superficial or external checklists cannot measure it.

# Groups: The Life-Giving Power of Community

I f you had to answer in a single word what God's dream for human beings is, what would you say?

Consider the word *community.*

Community is not a human invention. It is not a mere social phenomenon. Community is God's dearest creation. It is only within community that there is the possibility of knowing and being known, loving and being loved, serving and being served, celebrating and being celebrated.

Because God is community—Father, Son, and Spirit in oneness of being—he creates community. It flows from who he is. When God created the first being, he astoundingly declared his creation to be "not good" because it was solitary; so he created a partner. God's supreme achievement was not the creation of a solitary man but the creation of human community.

However, because of sin, God's ideal of community often seemed to have been lost. Many times, it hung only by a thin thread of hope. If God were a quitter, it might have ended altogether. But over the rubble of failed human community stands the towering form of the cross.

The very shape of the cross suggests the two main transactions that were effected through it. The upright post stands for the restoration of our community with God. God reached down from the holiness of his transcendence above, into the abyss of our human need in order to reconcile us to himself, through Christ. It reflects God's forgiving grace extended to receptive sinners. But the vertical trunk itself does not make a cross; it also requires a crossbar. The arms of Jesus were stretched on that horizontal beam, and his servant hands nailed to it. His extended arms reach out from the crossbar to all who want reconciliation with God in order that we may also be reconciled to one another, forming one body in his embrace of love.

Perfect community is to be found at the intersection of the two segments of the cross, where those who are reconciled with God are reconciled together—where we love God with all we have and we love our neighbor as ourselves. It is where we learn to care and share, to challenge and support, to confide and confess, to forgive and be forgiven, to laugh and weep, to be accountable to each other, to watch over each other, to be servants together. It is the place of transformation.

Community. It alone will survive from this world into the next. Then God's dream will be fulfilled when the church is eternally united as a bride to her husband in the Savior's embrace of redemptive love.

Will you be a part of building God's dream?

—Gilbert Bilezikian

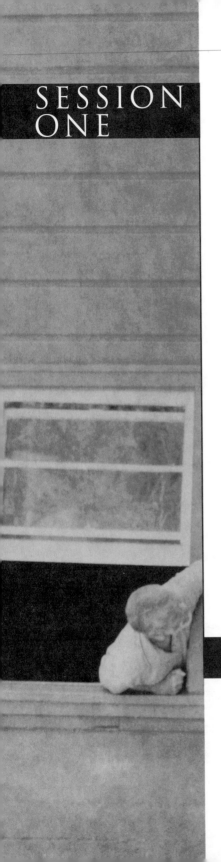

# SESSION
# ONE

# *This Is a Friendship*

Reading adapted from a message by Bill Hybels

There is a great story that dates back to the early 1960s when Vince Lombardi took over the reins of the Green Bay Packers. Most likely you've heard it before. It's become legendary. The Packer franchise had been losing for almost ten straight years. They were at the bottom of the standings, and morale was sagging.

*Every once in a while, we all need a breathtakingly basic talk about something.*

Enter Vince Lombardi as the new coach. He is charged with the challenge of turning this franchise around, and he's all pumped up about it. He began leading practices, inspiring, training, motivating. But at one point in a practice, he just got so frustrated with what was going on with the players that he blew the whistle.

"Everybody stop and gather around," he said. Then he knelt down, picked up the pigskin, and said, "Let's start at the beginning. This is a football. These are the yard markers. I'm the coach. You are the players." He went on, in the most elementary of ways, to explain the basics of football.

Every once in a while, we all need a breathtakingly basic talk about something—a "this is a football" talk or, in this case, a "this is a friendship" talk.

## The Right Idea

The Bible says that friendship—community—is one of the richest experiences you can have in life. It makes your heart bigger. It helps keep you steady in a storm. It ends your aloneness. It is key to personal transformation.

God wired us up to know and be known, to love and be loved, to serve and be served, to celebrate and be celebrated. If community is so wonderful, how, in painstakingly basic terms, do you move from where you are now into deep relating patterns that would fit the definition of this thing called community?

You have to start by making sure that you have the right idea about the nature of friendship. Do you want to wreck the possibility of a relationship? Then go into it with the idea that there's someone out there just sitting on a park bench waiting to nurture you, affirm you, comfort you, envelop you with round-the-clock care—and all you have to do is show up with 150 pounds of need. If that's the expectation you are bringing into friendship, you'll probably find potential friends making themselves curiously scarce.

*God wired us up to know and be known, to love and be loved, to serve and be served, to celebrate and be celebrated.*

The right idea of friendship involves the *mutual* exchange of knowledge, kindness, service, and celebration. It is a growing commitment among peers to seek the well-being of each other. That very radical concept is the central message of Philippians 2:1–11. The core of biblical friendship is seeking the interest of the person you have befriended. It is the joyful sublimation of your own agenda once in a while for the sheer pleasure of meeting a need or bringing a smile to the face of a friend. It is the consistent resistance of the urge to be independent and self-preoccupied.

Is it self-examination time? How much do you bring to the relationships you're building? How much do you expect to receive? What is your self-preoccupation factor? If you are even five or ten percent off from a balanced view of friendship, you'll probably find your relationships aren't working all that well.

### The "Want To" Factor

The next step in moving from aloneness to community is to face a sobering reality about the friendship-building process. Selecting and building friendships is an inexact and often lengthy, frustrating endeavor. It requires energy, risk, and, quite possibly, hurt. That is the plain truth.

When the Bible says that certain friends bring words that are comparable to silver and gold, it is certainly underscoring that friends are valuable. They have worth. But in addition to this, the friendship-development process itself might be compared to panning for silver and gold. You've got to work at it. Sometimes when you are mining for silver or gold, you think you have found it and you get all excited about it only to find out it's "fool's gold." Then you're let down and hurt.

There is a price to be paid up front for the eventual discovery of the mother lode—this thing called community. We would prefer a drive-up window. We would much rather pull up to the deep friendship window and say, "I want two, with change back from my dollar." Most of the time life doesn't work that way.

Community building is not easy. Very seldom can you just get plunked into a premade group and immediately experience community without some awkwardness, some trial and error. There has to be an internal "want to" factor that is strong enough to be able to push you through the false starts and stops that are going to happen as you build community.

*Very seldom can you just get plunked into a premade group and immediately experience community without some awkwardness, some trial and error.*

## Moving toward Authenticity

The next challenge you'll face in your quest for community is to move beyond the level of superficiality. When you start developing a relationship, you generally start out with conversations that are a bit shallow. And that is as it should be. Trust has to be built. The basic knowledge-base concerning one another must develop. But if you stay stuck at the superficial level—where all you're talking about is the weather, the stock market, and what movie you rented last weekend—you will probably start to say, "I was created for more than this."

Most of us get tired of surface relationships and wish we could move on. But how? The single best tool I have discovered to move relationships beyond the level of yawning superficiality is the asking of a carefully thought-out question and the urging of an honest, sincere answer.

What question do we ask almost everybody whenever we see them? "How are you doing?" The standard answers usually are, "Fine," "Good," or "Not bad."

What if you asked the question this way, "How are you doing, *really?*" "How are you doing, really—because I have a few moments and would love to listen to whatever it is that you'd like to talk about. How are things at work, really? How are things at home, really?"

I've asked that question and have sensed people say inside, "I think he means it." And they get tender. They want to open up. They just need to be given permission. That question has prompted hundreds of soulful conversations.

*What if you asked the question this way, "How are you doing, really?"*

There is another question that I'm beginning to use—it's the simple question, "How did you feel about that?" For example, you are waiting impatiently to start your golf game. Your friend is late. When he shows up you say, "Where were you?"

"I got stuck at work. Actually, my boss just raged all over me."

What is the normal response? "Sorry. Rage happens. Let's go—we'll miss our tee-off time." But what would happen if your follow-up question was, "Well, how did you feel about that?"

Another question I use a lot, especially with my kids, is, "What are you thinking right now?" It's more than a request for information. It is a statement of love. It's a way of saying, "Whatever is important to you right now—whatever is on your mind—is important to me. I want to know it."

These questions need to be asked at appropriate times in discerning ways. If people are reluctant to answer, you probably shouldn't press. But you've sent a clear message that you care, that you'll listen. They are the kinds of questions that prepare the soil for progressively deep kinds of sharing.

## The Key to Relational Freedom

Finally, your ability to experience and enjoy the fullness of human community is directly linked to the quality of your community with God.

Do you know the truth we never confess to? We all walk around wishing someone was thinking about us all the time—wishing that someone would move toward us with love all the time, be there for us all the time. We wish we were the center of someone's world. We put pressure on friendships that they weren't meant to bear. We raise the expectations higher and higher and people begin staying away.

Enter God. God says, "I have love of another kind. I have a lavish, uncontaminated, focused affection for you. I am thinking about you all the time. I am moving toward you with love all the time. I will be there for you all the time." When you open your heart up to the love of God through Christ, that love becomes the bedrock foundation out of which you move in your human relationships.

If your relationship with God is maturing, it gives you the inner security to take risks in human relationships. If a risk doesn't work out, you have not lost everything. You are not going to die. You have God's friendship in your life. From that rich point of security and peace you can move more freely in your relational world. You will grow into a more consistently loving person. You will develop deep community because you won't need it in the ultimate sense. You won't press for it in unhealthy ways or make demands that it can't deliver. You'll be positioned to experience it as a gift.

"This is a football." "This is a friendship." Let's be clear about it, move toward it, persevere in it. Let's offer good gifts of community to one another.

*When you open your heart up to the love of God through Christ, that love becomes the bedrock foundation out of which you move in your human relationships.*

# SPIRITUAL EXERCISE

I n Scripture we're told that Abraham, the great hero of faith, was given an amazing title. God called him "my friend" (Isa. 41:8). Even more amazing, Jesus told his followers that he no longer called them his servants but rather his friends (John 15:15). His enemies gave Jesus the title "friend of . . . 'sinners'" (Matt. 11:19), intending it as an insult. Instead, he wore it as a badge of honor.

Jesus not only wants to be your Savior, Teacher, and Lord, he longs to be your friend. Devote this week to cultivating a deeper friendship with Jesus. Consciously seek his companionship. Enjoy his presence. Share your life, thoughts, and activities with him as true friends do together. Here are some ideas:

- When you wake up, remember that Jesus is present with you as a friend. You are already on his mind. Invite him to spend the day with you.
- Throughout the day, whenever you are tempted, anxious, or discouraged, take that emotion as a cue to remind you that you are not alone. Take a moment to talk to Jesus about your concern, as one friend would speak to another.
- At some point during the day, take time out to do something you love to do. It may be taking a walk, listening to music, riding a motorcycle, or pursuing a hobby. Invite Jesus to be a part of this activity. Don't strain yourself to pray or to make the time be "spiritual." Simply be aware that he is with you as your friend. Speak to him as it feels natural to do so.
- When something good happens—even if it seems small or insignificant—express your gratitude or joy to Jesus. Take a moment to reflect that he shares your joy with you, as any good friend does.
- When someone else's need interrupts your day, seize it as an opportunity to serve Jesus as you would do a favor for a good friend.

Keep track of how this exercise goes. How hard is it for you to relate to Jesus as a trusted friend? What difference does it make in your life as you stretch yourself to experience him in that way?

We can learn much about authentic Christian community from the apostle Paul. Both his life experiences and his explicit instructions about relationships have given believers a wonderful picture of how the body of Christ is supposed to operate—how important relationships are, how to strengthen them, and how to work through inevitable difficulties.

But Paul was not always a passionate builder of community. The first mention of Paul (then named Saul) is in Acts 7. The scene is the trial of Stephen, who was falsely arrested for allegedly teaching against Moses and God. At the end of the trial, Stephen is martyred by stoning. Read the account in Acts 7:54–8:3.

1. What was Saul's attitude about the death of Stephen?




What additional actions did Saul take against Christians?




2. What insight does Paul's own description of his preconversion condition give you concerning what he was like and what was important to him at that time? (See Phil. 3:4–6; Gal.1:13–14; Acts 22:1–5)

NOTE: Paul describes himself as zealous for God. "Zeal" is a significant term to help us understand the preconversion Paul. In his book *What Paul Really Said,* scholar N. T. Wright observes, "Whereas for the modern Christian 'zeal' is something you do on your knees, or in evangelism, or in works of charity, for the first-century Jew 'zeal' was something you did with a knife. Those first-century Jews who longed for revolution against Rome . . . saw themselves . . . as having the right, and the duty, to put that zeal into operation with the use of violence. 'Zeal' thus comes close to holy war. . . ."

3. Acts 9 describes Paul's dramatic conversion. Through that singular encounter with Christ, Paul's passions were forever redirected, his priorities forever changed. From the following passages (all excerpts from letters Paul wrote to various young churches), how is that redirection seen, particularly when it comes to relationships and community?

Philippians 4:1

Colossians 2:1 – 5

1 Thessalonians 2:7 – 8, 11 – 12, 17 – 20

Acts 20:36 – 38 (Paul's farewell to the elders of the church at Ephesus)

4. Paul knew the importance of mutuality in relationships. Considering the following verses, how did Paul demonstrate that he possessed the grace to *give* as well as the grace to *receive* in relationships?

Romans 1:11–12

Romans 15:24, 30–32

Philippians 1:3–11

5. Read Paul's statements to his protégé Timothy in 2 Timothy 4:9–16. In what ways did Paul know relational disappointment?

When it came to building community, what do you think helped keep Paul's "want to" factor high, even in the face of such severe disappointments?

6. Paul also built relationships by pressing on and revealing his heart and emotions—not just remaining superficial. How does he show his openness and vulnerability in the following passages?

Romans 7:14−25

2 Corinthians 6:11−13

1 Timothy 1:12–17

Paul made the transition in his life to the place where relationships were extremely significant and precious to him. He was transformed from being mostly concerned with zeal and the pursuit of his own agenda, to being mostly concerned with love, the spreading of God's grace, and the building of Christian community. With Paul's transformation as a backdrop, let's take the pulse of your own relational world.

7. To what extent do you relate to Paul's experience of community? In what ways is it most foreign?

8. To what degree do you identify with his experience of transformation? Have there been any defining moments or eras when you changed from zealously pursuing your own private agenda to zealously pursuing relationships and Christian community?

9. Check the statements below that apply to you, and indicate why:

_____ Sometimes I seem to have enough friends, and other times I feel lonely.

_____ I have lots of friends, but we don't seem to get very deep.

_____ I have only a few friends, but our relationships are very rich.

_____ I have had to really work at making friendships.

_____ I have tried over and over again to have meaningful friendships, but it never works out.

_____ I have never had what you would call a "best friend."

Why:

10. When it comes to your relational "want to" factor, how would you describe yourself right now?

_____ I have lots of energy for making my relationships better

_____ I want to improve my relationships, though sometimes it drains me

_____ I'm not sure I'm up for any new relational challenges

_____ I am weary of trying to work on relationships

Additional observations:

11. How is your friendship with God these days?

_____ I regularly experience rich friendship with God

_____ Sometimes I can sense God's friendship, but not always

_____ I really don't think much about God being my friend

_____ I am not comfortable with the thought of God as my friend

Additional observations:

12. As you walk into a typical small group meeting, you may be rehearsing what you are going to say and how others may respond. You may be wondering if the experience will be satisfying or whether the meeting will go by without you getting your needs met. On each continuum below, mark where you see yourself:

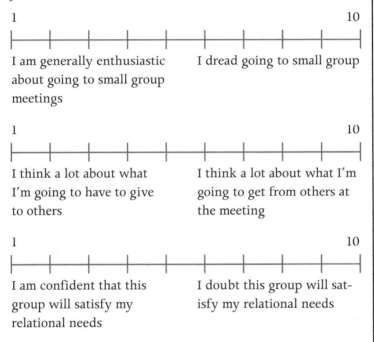

1                                                                    10

I am generally enthusiastic          I dread going to small group
about going to small group
meetings

1                                                                    10

I think a lot about what             I think a lot about what I'm
I'm going to have to give            going to get from others at
to others                            the meeting

1                                                                    10

I am confident that this             I doubt this group will sat-
group will satisfy my                isfy my relational needs
relational needs

---

NOTE: A small group is a wonderful place for life-change and, outside of a family, perhaps the most optimal setting for personal transformation. But groups are imperfect, as are the people in them. This reality, if not recognized, can set a person up for deep disappointment because we often hope our small group will be the place where we finally find this wonderful thing called community, yet our experience can fall short. It is important not to put too much pressure on any one group— or on the members of your group (including the leader)—to meet every need relationally or spiritually.

Each group you are a part of will contribute to your growth. Over the years, you'll build many good memories. But every person in your group is not going to become a friend for life. That doesn't mean you can't love each other and meaningfully contribute to each other while you are together, but it does mean it's important to accept the limitations of each group, and recognize there is an ebb and flow to relationships.

Also, we each bring our own "baggage" to the group. Part of why God wants us in groups is so that we can deal with these problems. Of course, no group is going to solve everything for us. Similarly, a small group can be the place where you move toward a person with whom you wouldn't normally associate—someone different than you, or who has different interests, and with whom you have to work to make the group go. A challenging relationship can be as powerfully transforming as a relationship that happens almost without effort—maybe more so.

As you look to your expectations for this group, go ahead and plan for great things, but realize that it's community over a lifetime that helps make us like Jesus. Be ready at times to give more than you receive. And don't place on any one person or group the expectation for community that is possible only from years of group life.

13. What would you like to see as some group goals during this seven-session study on relationships? Be as specific as you can.

# TAKE-AWAY

*My summary of the main point of this session, and how it impacts me personally:*

NOTE: You will fill in this information after your group discussion. Leave it blank until the conclusion of your meeting.

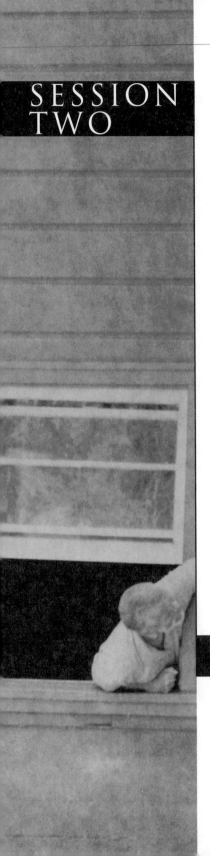

# SESSION TWO

LOVE PAYS ATTENTION

# *Love Pays Attention*

Reading adapted from a message by John Ortberg

It's a common scene. A couple sits at the breakfast table. One spouse (let's say the husband) is immersed in the newspaper, while the wife is pouring out her heart. Frustrated, she finally complains, "You're not listening to me."

"I can repeat every word you said," is the standard response. He proceeds to demonstrate. Is she satisfied? No! She doesn't want him simply to be able to replay her words. A tape recorder could do that. She wants him to be fully present. She wants him to put down the paper, look her in the eye, and pay attention to her.

Being heard is not enough. She wants to be *attended to*.

Attention is one of the most powerful forces in the world. Along with food and water, a baby needs to see the attentive gaze of a human face to develop properly. When we grow up, we still need to be attended to.

I went to graduate school for several years to learn about clinical psychology. There was one thing I learned quickly. The thing people value as much as direction or insight when they go to someone for counseling is to be in the presence of another human being who will actually look at them, listen to them, pay attention to them, and treat their lives and hearts as though they mattered.

God's greatest commandment for building community is "love one another." A primary work of love is paying attention. It is such a valuable thing that we don't just give it — we *pay* it. It's like money.

*Attention is one of the most powerful forces in the world.*

### The Attentive Face of God

One of the great miracles of life is that God pays attention to us. This is partly why the writers of Scripture speak so often of God's face. The great priestly blessing that God himself taught the people of Israel says: "The LORD bless you and keep you; the LORD make his face shine upon you and be gracious to you; the LORD turn his face toward you and give you peace" (Num. 6:24–26).

To turn your face toward someone is to give them your wholehearted, undivided attention. It is not the casual listening of a preoccupied mind. It is a statement saying, "I have nothing else to do, nowhere I'd rather be. I'm fully devoted to being with you." This is the kind of attention God devotes to us.

The priestly blessing says that God will not only turn his face toward us, he will make it *shine* on us. The shining face is an image of delight. It is the face of a proud parent beaming while a child plays in his first piano recital. It is the radiant face of a groom as he watches his bride walk the aisle. Faces that shine and grow radiant only happen in the presence of the deepest kind of love.

*Faces that shine and grow radiant only happen in the presence of the deepest kind of love.*

This is how God loves us. God pays attention to us. To lose God's loving attention was, to the psalmist, to lose everything:

> *My heart says of you, "Seek his face!" Your face, LORD, I will seek. Do not hide your face from me, do not turn your servant away in anger; you have been my helper. Do not reject me, or forsake me, O God my Savior!*
>
> —Psalm 27:8–9

Nothing was worse than the thought of God hiding his face.

God pays attention. Close attention. "The very hairs of your head are all numbered," Jesus said (Luke 12:7). We often take it as a sign of love if someone is able to notice a haircut or change in hairstyle. Marriages have been known to break up over the *failure* to notice. God has numbered every hair! If one falls out, he notices. He may not replace it, unfortunately, but he notices. Jesus is not teaching here about God's capacity to process information or crunch numbers. He is teaching that God is infinitely attentive to even the smallest details of our lives.

God pays attention.

## Attending to People

What does it mean for you to pursue the work of God? It is to grow to see as he sees, listen as he listens, attend as he attends to the people in your relational world. But what, specifically, does attentive love do?

*Love remembers.* What's his favorite movie? What kind of coffee does she like? When is his birthday? Love recalls the significant events that happened in a friend's life last week. Love remembers a loss that was suffered a year ago on this day. Love is in the details.

*God has numbered every hair! If one falls out, he notices. He may not replace it, unfortunately, but he notices.*

*Love notices.* In her book *You Just Don't Understand,* Deborah Tannen tells the story of her great-aunt, who had a romantic relationship when she was in her seventies. Obese, balding, misshapen by arthritis, she did not fit the stereotype of a woman romantically loved. But she was. By a man who also was in his seventies.

> One evening she had dinner out, with friends. When she returned home, her male friend called and she told him about the dinner. He listened with interest and asked her, "What did you wear?" When she told me this, she began to cry: "Do you know how many years it's been since anyone asked me what I wore?"
>
> When my great-aunt said this, she was saying that it had been years since anyone cared deeply — intimately — about her.

If you want to do the work of God, pay attention to people. Notice them. Observe them. Take time to highlight what you find attractive, winsome, praiseworthy. We have the power to delight each other's hearts when we notice and celebrate each other.

*Love listens*. There are people around you today who need more than anything else for you to "put down the newspaper" and pay attention. When you are sitting around the kitchen table or within the circle of your small group and someone speaks, "turn your face" to them. Look them in the eye. Give them your undivided attention. Be fully present with them for that moment—even if it's only a moment. Listen to the words of their mouth. Listen to the words of their heart.

An amazing thing happens as we become more intentional about attending to people. We become a little more able to attend to God. Slowing down, being fully present, focusing, listening. They are the same skills needed to deal with our own *spiritual* attention deficit disorder. As we grow in our ability to attend to people, there's a good chance we will grow in our ability to attend to the "still, small voice" of God.

Paying attention is a powerful thing. It can transform relationships. It can transform our hearts. "Let anyone with ears listen," Jesus would often say.

Pay attention!

*Listen to the words of their heart.*

# SPIRITUAL EXERCISE

Your exercise this week is simply to *listen*. Attending to people with a responsive heart is one of the most concrete ways to express Christ's love. Through various encounters this week — whether momentary or substantial — practice the discipline of listening. In doing so, consider the following:

- When a person is talking, make eye contact. Literally, "turn your face toward them." Give them your full attention.
- Make every effort to be fully present in the conversation. If your mind starts racing to other things you must do, just *stop*. Remind yourself that this moment — even if it's only a moment — is a powerful opportunity to love as Jesus loved.
- Commit, at least for this week, that you will not interrupt.
- Try to enter into the person's experience as you listen. What are the feelings behind the words? Consider asking, if appropriate, "How did you feel about that?" or a similar question that reflects genuine interest.
- Resist the temptation to formulate what *you'll* say next while the other person is speaking. If there's a pause in the conversation, avoid shifting the focus to yourself. Stay with the person and their story.
- As you listen to another person, listen with a "third ear" — one attuned to the Holy Spirit. What might God be saying to you through this person? What might God want to say to this person through you?

Once each day, pause to jot down some observations. How hard is it to stay fully focused on someone else? Are you finding it more difficult with some people than others? How often do you find yourself subtly (or not so subtly) bringing the conversation around to yourself? How did different people respond to your listening? How are you being impacted personally?

1. God is the supreme example of one who pays careful attention. Few passages of Scripture express this truth more powerfully than David's Psalm 139. Read through this psalm several times. Then put in your own words all the ways God demonstrates his loving attentiveness.

2. Jesus also taught about God's life-giving attention toward us. How would you summarize God's mindfulness of the details of our lives according to these verses?

   Matthew 6:25–33

   Matthew 10:29–31

3. Was there a time recently when you strongly felt the attentiveness of God toward you—a time when he was particularly mindful of some detail in your life? What impact did that experience have on you?

4. Sometimes we feel great disappointment when God *doesn't* seem to be paying attention. In Psalm 42:9–10, the psalmist also feels uncared for by God. Describe a time when you felt like God wasn't paying attention to you.

In times like this, why do we need more than just the theological understanding that God knows all about our circumstances? What is the deeper need?

Now read verse 11 of Psalm 42. What do you suppose helps someone come to the place of trust even in the midst of questioning God's presence, as the psalmist does here?

5. Sometimes we forget that God has feelings too. Consider again these words from the reading:

Love notices
Love remembers
Love listens

How have you expressed loving attentiveness to *God* in these areas during the past month?

6. Peter and John came across a handicapped man one day by the temple (Acts 3:1–10). They eventually healed him. But what was the first act of compassion they showed to this man?

What effect would this action have on a person who was used to being avoided and treated as invisible?

Can you think of any people in your life who you sometimes treat as invisible or take for granted? What could you do to pay better attention to them?

7. One of the men Paul invested his life in was a young pastor named Timothy. Based on the following passages (taken from two letters that Paul wrote to Timothy), how do you see Paul's loving attention expressed regarding Timothy's spiritual development? Regarding possible insecurities? Health issues? The need for affirmation and affection? What indications are there that Timothy paid attention to some of Paul's unique needs?

1 Timothy 1:1−2

1 Timothy 4:12−16

1 Timothy 5:23

1 Timothy 6:11−12

2 Timothy 1:1−9

2 Timothy 4:9, 13, 21

8. Spend some time reflecting on your significant relationships. On a scale of 1–5 (1 being low and 5 being high), how do you rate your present attentiveness level (noticing, remembering, listening)?

\_\_\_ Close friends
\_\_\_ Small group members
\_\_\_ Family members
\_\_\_ Others

What observations can you make about the way you rated yourself? Is there consistency, or are some scores significantly higher or lower than others?

Do you have any sense of what might be contributing to these patterns?

Do you sense the Spirit's prompting regarding any of these relationships?

Consider taking a risk. If it feels appropriate, ask the individuals for their assessment. How closely does it match your own?

9. How well would you say your small group is doing when it comes to attending to one another? What improvements, if any, would you constructively suggest?

NOTE: From time to time, we meet people who seem to demand constant attention. For such folks, no amount of caring seems enough. Is it the Christlike thing to keep pouring on more attention?

This situation is very difficult to handle, and requires discernment. Certainly, every person's pain should be heard. But sometimes, the attention demanded is actually a way to avoid entering a more difficult process of finding out how to really solve the problem. In those cases, the person's request for help is actually a diversion from the real issue. When confronted, the person may become very defensive, or go into an even more pronounced victim role. What is usually true is that the person won't take responsibility for change. They would rather repeat a pattern of focusing everyone's attention on themselves, their plight, the unfairness of those around them, and—here's the tough part to respond to appropriately—everybody else's responsibility to care for them. Listeners who want to model Christlike love can become hooked and think that the solution is more attention, more rescuing, more of whatever the person is asking for.

It's probably best, when in doubt about a person's true needs, to err on the side of nonjudgmental empathy. But there will come a time when truth needs to be spoken in love. Encourage the person to talk to a good Christian counselor who can help uncover the deeper issues keeping the person stuck. Be prepared not just to pay attention but to pay the right kind of attention. That's how to live as if Jesus were in your place with every person you meet.

# TAKE-AWAY

*My summary of the main point of this session, and how it impacts me personally:*

NOTE: You will fill in this information after your group discussion. Leave it blank until the conclusion of your meeting.

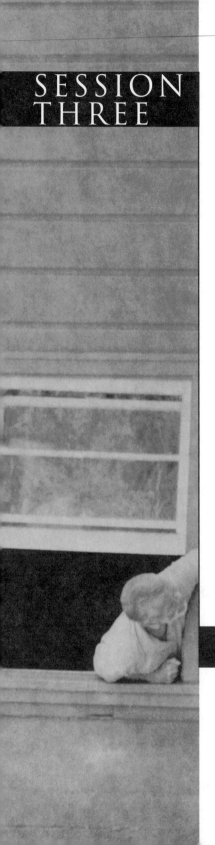

# SESSION
# THREE

# KNOWING
# AND BEING KNOWN

# SESSION THREE

## *Knowing and Being Known*

Reading adapted from a message by John Ortberg

We want to be known, but we want to hide. A friend of mine wrote of a recent experience:

*We shook hands warmly before leaving the restaurant. I had a great time meeting with this man. A true brotherhood was developing. That's why what he said was so shocking.*

*"I'm really enjoying getting to know you," he said. I smiled my approval. Then he added, "It's been especially good to see your human side."*

*My "human side"? Just what else was there to see?*

*He left before my bewilderment could blossom into more conversation. But for days to come, I kept returning to that phrase, "It's been especially good to see your human side."*

*His words stung. They made me face the truth about my "fence"—the impressions I hide behind. It's an internal electrified barrier energized by the 10,000-volt certainty that I need this protection. If people see the untamed part of me, I'm sure I'll be rejected.*

*And yet my friend was glad to see the power turned off and the gate opened a bit. He actually preferred my rough-edged humanity. All that work to construct a secure enclosure, yet when I let him inside, he didn't reject me. With the barrier down, I moved toward*

> We want to be known, but we want to hide.

*the very friendship I thought only the barrier made possible.*

*Go figure.*

## Why We Hide

I'd like to say that I can't identify with my friend, but I can—more than I want to admit. We live in a world where image projection and impression management is the rule of thumb, and it gets inside everyone of us. I know that as a teacher I want to be honest and open, but there is such a strong tendency to hide and to want to look better than I am. This truth about me comes out in unguarded moments.

Several years ago I was with one of my kids in Wisconsin. We were at a store and this particular child kept pestering me for a toy. Finally, my anger boiled over. "No, I'm not going to get you that toy. I'm not going to get it for you today. I'm not going to get it for you tomorrow. I'm not going to get it next month or next year. I am *never* going to get it for you! Do you understand? *When you're seventy and I'm a hundred years old, I'm still not going to get it for you!*"

Just that moment the clerk looked at me and said, "You look awfully familiar. Do you teach at Willow Creek Community Church?"

I said, "Yes, my name is Bill Hybels." I didn't really say that, but I wanted to. I wanted to hide. It was awful.

*There is a high cost to hiding. If I hide, sin wins.*

## The High Cost of Hiding

We'll never fully experience community or significant transformation until we begin to acknowledge to others the truth about ourselves. Ironically, churches are often the last place this happens. Consider these words from Richard Foster's book *Celebration of Discipline:*

> *Confession is so difficult a Discipline for us partly because we view the believing community as a fellowship of saints before we see it as a fellowship of sinners. We come to feel that everyone else has*

*advanced so far into holiness that we are isolated and alone in our sin. . . . We imagine that we are the only ones who have not stepped onto the high road to heaven. Therefore we hide ourselves from one another and live in veiled lies and hypocrisy. . . .*

There is a high cost to hiding. If I hide, my relationships become stagnant. If I hide, others are likely to hide too. If I hide, I can never know I'm loved unconditionally. If I hide, sin wins. If I hide, I lose the help I might receive for secret struggles and hurts.

### God's Plan for Community

God says an amazing thing: "In my community, there should be no more hiding, no more masks. My community is just people—every one of whom struggles with sin and does stupid things and says foolish things and then comes to me and confesses, gets back up, moves forward and then fouls up again. People don't have to pretend they're something they're not. I intend for people to live in the light."

James says it this way: "Therefore confess your sins to each other and pray for each other so that you may be healed" (James 5:16). James is talking about living in authentic, open community. Confession involves acknowledging the truth about my life—the negative as well as the positive—to God, to myself, and, in appropriate ways, to brothers and sisters in the body.

Humanity is no longer denied but transformed through community. That is God's plan. Every time there is a great movement of God throughout the history of the church, one of the things that happens is that people get serious about this business of confession and they acknowledge to God, to themselves, and to other people the truth about their lives. There is enormous power when we come into the light.

### Step by Step

In true community, self-disclosure can't be forced. It can't and shouldn't be manipulated or pressured so that

*Humanity is no longer denied but transformed through community.*

people say things in inappropriate settings or ways. "Confess your sins to one another" does not mean you reveal all of your sins to everyone in the church—probably not even to everyone in your small group. A realistic goal would be to move progressively toward the establishment of one or two relationships in which you can talk about everything in your life.

In pursuit of that goal, there is a natural progression that healthy relationships tend to follow. At the first level, conversation remains pretty safe. It might include discussing ordinary events such as work and recreation, topics we tend to agree on.

At level two things begin to get deeper. We begin to express strong opinions and significant feelings. We risk disagreeing with each other.

The third level encompasses our deeper secrets, struggles, and temptations even though we have not overcome them yet. It is at this level we feel secure enough in the relationship to reveal shame and guilt from our past. We are open about dreams and failures.

Self-disclosure, especially at level three, must be done wisely and with discernment. It is generally not smart to plunge into it all at once. Trust must be established over time. Take a relatively small risk and see how the person responds. Gradually open the door. As a general rule, the deeper the level of brokenness that you intend to share, the more you need to be sure that the one you tell is a mature believer who you know and trust deeply. This person should be a supportive person—someone who empathizes with your situation and who will appropriately honor confidentiality.

### It's Up to You

It's possible for people to attend the same church—even the same small group—sit in the same chair, nod to the same people, talk about sports, the weather, or even the Bible month after month, year after year, without anyone ever knowing them. Nobody knows their hopes, their

*"Confess your sins to one another" does not mean you reveal all of your sins to everyone in the church.*

fears. Nobody knows their marriage is crumbling, their heart is breaking. Nobody knows they are involved in a secret pattern of sin that is destroying their soul. This is not God's plan. It's a mockery of community.

Ultimately, only you can decide if you are going to come out of hiding. You don't *have* to do it. Nobody will force you to do it. You can maintain your reputation. You can cultivate your impression management. You can protect your status. Or you can come into the light. You can know and be known. You can move toward healing and transformation. You can know the kind of community that can only happen among forgiven sinners.

It's up to you.

# BIBLE STUDY

One way to picture the various relational spheres in which God works to transform us is with a series of concentric circles. At the very core is our individual connection with God. Outside that central relationship are one-on-one relationships with individuals who mentor or encourage us and with whom we do likewise—what we might call "spiritual friendships." The next sphere is a group of four to ten people gathering regularly—in other words, a small group. Then God uses large meetings, such as weekend and midweek services, where we are part of a much bigger community.

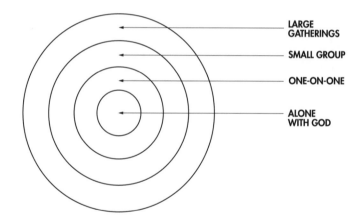

Each sphere has its own benefits and limitations. Clearly, we need each type of relational environment in order to experience the fullness of God's work in our lives, including our growth in knowing and being known.

## Alone with God

1. Dietrich Bonhoeffer, the German pastor martyred by Hitler, wrote, "Let him who cannot be alone beware of community." What do you think Bonhoeffer meant by that warning? Why are our private times with God so essential—even to the building of community?

2. Ever since the Garden of Eden, humans have tried to hide from God when they feel ashamed. David was no stranger to this tendency. According to Psalm 32:3–4, what are the by-products of such hiding?

3. Take inventory of your own life during the past month:

   What have been your points of greatest temptation or struggle?

What hidden faults have reared their head? (Pride? Envy? Lust? Greed? A critical spirit?)

Have you hurt anyone with your actions?

In what way have you been trying to hide any of these realities from God? Have you noticed any of the by-products of hiding as David did in Psalm 32?

Now read Psalm 32:5. What would it take for you right now to be able to say these same words? What is God's promised response?

4. Second Samuel 11 records the most notorious time when David sinned and orchestrated a cover-up. After committing adultery with a married woman, Bathsheba, David deliberately ordered her husband, Uriah, to be killed (v. 15). But Nathan, a friend of David, knew the truth. What difficult and courageous action did Nathan take? (2 Sam. 12:1–7)

What was the result? (v. 13)

Do you have any "Nathans" in your life? When was the last time a friend lovingly spoke difficult truth to you?

5. No one enjoys having someone expose something we'd rather leave hidden. Being honest, what negative responses are you most inclined to when you are confronted?

_____ I get angry

_____ I defend my actions

_____ I withdraw from the person

_____ I feel sorry for myself and pout

_____ I deny the problem is mine and blame others

_____ I outwardly comply, but feel resentful

_____ Other:

Why do you think this is so? What emotions are kindled when something in you is being exposed?

6. When the time comes for *you* to be a "Nathan," what attitude and approach does Paul instruct us to have and why?

Galatians 6:1–2

Ephesians 4:15, 29

7. Why do these kind of confrontations generally happen better in one-on-one settings than in group settings?

## Small Group

8. If close one-on-one relationships are so vital, you might think that they are all that's necessary for spiritual health. But that is not so. Consider Solomon's words in Proverbs 27:17. How do you think the sharpening that Solomon speaks of can actually be *heightened* in a small group setting? How does the diversity represented in the group impact this?

9. God has created us all very differently. Your small group likely includes certain people who magnify those differences. You may have someone in your group who you don't even like. How could that still lead to the sharpening work of God?

NOTE: When it comes to building community, it is important to remember that the goal is not solely the development of rich, satisfying relationships. How God transforms us in the process is as important as the end product. Our spiritual development can be furthered every bit as much through difficult, even painful, relational situations as it can through the easy, joy-producing ones—if we are willing to continually ask the question, "How can this situation change me to live more like Jesus?"

10. Consider the times when others in your group have allowed themselves to come out of hiding and be known. Are there any specific ways in which you have been sharpened spiritually just by hearing their journey through struggles, weakness, and failures?

11. Consider this statement from Robert Mulholland's *Invitation to a Journey:* "The process of being conformed to the image of Christ takes place primarily at the points of our *unlikeness* to Christ's image" (italics added). How would you explain the meaning of that statement?

In light of this, why is it so important to get a clear picture of our own areas of sin, weakness, and immaturity?

What role can small group members play in helping diagnose our need and move beyond self-deception?

12. In order to further the goal of knowing and being known, be prepared to respond to one of these questions in your next group meeting:

What is one thing a lot of people assume about you that you honestly wish they wouldn't?

What is one of your greatest personal desires for the year?

What is one of your greatest fears?

**Large Gatherings**

13. Finally, God uses large gatherings of the Body to further our spiritual transformation. Acts 2:14–36 describes the first public service after Jesus' resurrection when Peter proclaimed the gospel. According to verse 37, what effect did it have?

Have you ever experienced the cutting, exposing work of the Spirit when you were gathered with the body for teaching? Describe it.

14. How does God use large group worship times to further your growth in ways that probably wouldn't happen except through such times?

NOTE: The next time you attend a teaching or worship service, consider taking your seat a few minutes early to prepare your heart and mind. Offer Psalm 139:23–24 as a prayer to God. Invite him to search you, know you, and lead you through the worship and teaching that you are about to experience.

*Search me, O God, and know my heart; test me and know my anxious thoughts. See if there is any offensive way in me, and lead me in the way everlasting.*

# SPIRITUAL EXERCISE

One of the most crushing forms of aloneness is to be alone in the knowledge of our sin, our guilt, our failures. To share these with a deeply trusted Christian friend or counselor can release the guilt, allow you to experience the freedom of being forgiven by God, and help you gain clarity of the ways to move toward change and growth.

Commit to pursuing one of the following next steps when it comes to "being known."

- If you cannot presently identify such a trusted Christian friend, commit to making that a matter of regular prayer. Pursue it. Ask God to help you search out that person or to help you further cultivate an existing friendship.

- If you believe you have someone in your life who could help you come into the light, schedule a time to meet with him or her. Your next step might be sharing with them one or two of the hidden faults or temptations that you identified in the "Alone with God" section of the Bible study. How did they respond? Is it with a balance of truth and grace? Does their feedback reflect wisdom and discernment? If so, ask if they would be willing to play this role on a more consistent basis. Give them permission to become a "Nathan" for you.

- If you are already in a relationship that has many years of trust and you feel full confidence in the relationship and the person's maturity, schedule a time when you can bring your entire life into the light with them—present sin, struggles, and secrets, as well as any that are still nagging you from the past. Some people do this by writing what it is that they want to confess on a sheet of paper (or several sheets, if necessary!) and then having their friend burn it as an expression of the triumph of God's forgiveness. In any case, be sure to allow the person time to respond and assure you of God's full forgiveness and ongoing support. Consider scheduling time on a periodic basis with your friend to stay current with issues and temptations.

NOTE: How do you become a safe person to someone who asks you to be their confidant? Probably one of the most crucial aspects is confidentiality (Prov. 11:13). If you are the type who can't resist the temptation to pass on sensitive information, don't receive a person's confession. On the other hand, be aware that no one should expect you to make unconditional promises of confidentiality. Destructive patterns of ongoing sin and refusal to take constructive steps may call for additional intervention.

In the spirit of Galatians 6:1 ("... watch yourself, or you also may be tempted"), be sure you are not coming off as arrogant. This is no time to pretend you're above temptation. Identify with the person. Even if the sin is not anything that attracts you, all of us know what it's like to do what we'd rather not (Rom. 7:15), so you've been there too. Listen thoughtfully, and don't rush to give advice. Don't worry about fixing the person at this point. He or she may need help in clarifying a constructive course of action, but don't rush into that before the pain and shame have been revealed and you've joined with the person's feelings.

You also become a safe person by caring enough to follow through. Future meetings, notes of encouragement, phone calls, prayer support, loving accountability—commit to whatever it takes to assure the person you will not only hear the problem but walk with them on the path toward freedom.

Sometimes your role will be to encourage a person to seek professional counseling. People can be reluctant to go to a counselor, but many times that is the most appropriate step to take. Let the person know there is no stigma attached to people who use the resources of a wise and competent Christian counselor. It will probably be greatly appreciated if you continue your support while the person works there too.

# TAKE-AWAY

*My summary of the main point of this session, and how it impacts me personally:*

NOTE: You will fill in this information after your group discussion. Leave it blank until the conclusion of your meeting.

# SESSION FOUR

## WHEN COMMUNITY BREAKS DOWN

# When Community Breaks Down

Reading adapted from a message by John Ortberg

I am mechanically dysfunctional—especially when it comes to cars. My theory is that all car engines are hypochondriacal. If you don't baby them every time they make a strange noise, they'll quit whining and get back to work.

Because I approach the life of my car this way, sometimes there is a complete breakdown. When that happens, I do what all men do. I get out of the car, raise the hood, and look inside. I have no idea why I do this. It's not as if there is just a big on-off switch under the hood, which I might be able to handle. I guess it makes me feel a bit better while waiting for the AAA guy. Invariably, he will end our time together with his encouraging words, "You know, this could have been prevented. Didn't you read your owner's manual?"

A lot of people approach a far more serious kind of breakdown—a relational breakdown—with not much more thoughtfulness than I tend to give to automotive breakdowns. So what do you do when you get stuck relationally? Jesus has given a set of instructions. It's in the "manual," recorded in Matthew 18:15. It can be summarized this way: *If another person wrongs you—when there is conflict—you go to the other person in private and discuss the problem for the purpose of reconciliation.*

Of all the teachings Jesus ever gave us, this may be the one that we most often violate. Because at every point

*Of all the teachings Jesus ever gave us, this may be the one that we most often violate. Because at every point in this teaching we are faced with a decision.*

in this teaching we are faced with a decision. And we have powerful reasons to ignore his instructions. Let's walk through Jesus' words so that we have absolute clarity as to what we are to do.

### Acknowledge the Conflict

The first step is something you do in your mind—acknowledge the conflict. People fight. Sometimes constructively, sometimes destructively. Sometimes fights end in hugs and kisses, sometimes they end in coldness and withdrawal.

To be alive means to be in conflict. For lots of reasons, it is easier to pretend that conflict does not exist. But entering into life in community will require a tenacious inner commitment that you will not live with unaddressed conflict. Let's start with a deep commitment to face relational breakdowns squarely in the eye.

### Take Initiative

Jesus is clear about the next step. If there is conflict, *you go. You* are to take initiative. But, chances are, you don't want to! "Let the other person come to me. Why do I always have to take the first step? Why can't she take the first step? Why does he always have to be so stubborn and mule-headed?"

Have you ever had those thoughts? Well, Jesus puts the burden on *you*—and he does it whether you are the one hurt or the one who did the hurting (Matt. 5:23–24). He says that *you* are to take action. Don't wait for the other person to step up to fix the problem.

You are to *go*. Once again, this is not something I want to do. I want to stay and stew. I'd rather just be mad. It's more fun to pout about conflict and rehearse the ways in which the other person unfairly hurt me. Besides, if I go, it may get ugly. If I go, it may be scary. Most of us fear confrontation.

The *go* step is a huge one. It's important to understand that you may not even do it terribly well. You may stum-

*But entering into life in community will require a tenacious inner commitment that you will not live with unaddressed conflict.*

PURSUING SPIRITUAL TRANSFORMATION

ble all over your words. It doesn't matter. Of course, it's important that you use as much skill and wisdom as you can, and it can be very helpful to plan ahead what you're going to say, but the main thing is not that you do it flawlessly. The main thing is that you *go,* because avoiding conflict kills community. Resentment builds up inside you like buried toxic waste. And sooner or later it will leak. Jesus says you must approach, not avoid.

### No Third Parties

So who do you go *to?* Jesus is clear. You go to the person with whom you have the conflict. This seems obvious. But usually this is the last person I want to go to. I want to go to somebody else—to a person who is not involved and say, "Don't you share my concerns about my brother in Christ who is obviously a deeply disturbed psychopath?" It's more fun to go to somebody else, because I can commiserate with them and get reinforcement for my anger. But the Bible says that is not the way to go.

In community, we all must be prepared in this regard. Sooner or later someone will come to *you* to complain about another person. It is often fun to hear their complaints. In a way, it can bond the two of you. But it's not helping the situation. So you need to think in advance of a gracious, tactful way of encouraging the person not to ventilate to you but to go to the one involved.

If you have thoughtfully and carefully confronted without good resolve, *then and only then* Jesus says to involve a few other mature believers in the process (Matt. 18:16).

### Direct Communication

Jesus says to go when the two of you are alone. This means you will have to avoid the temptation to embarrass the person in front of friends. Have you ever done that? Have you ever served up a well-placed jab in front of friends? Maybe it was done with humor, but it was still a jab. And it was in front of people. Jesus said to put aside any desire to embarrass the person. Go in private.

*So who do you go* to? *Jesus is clear. You go to the person with whom you have the conflict.*

Then Jesus says you are to discuss the problem. Talk about it. Engage in direct communication. Sometimes, in an effort to soften the blow, we end up addressing the problem indirectly. We talk around it. We avoid naming it. Sometimes we get manipulative and put it in the form of a question instead of a direct statement.

For instance, a wife says to her husband, "Wouldn't you like to get the garage cleaned up today?" He reflects on the state of his heart and discovers that, at the intimate core of who he is, he really would *not* like to get the garage cleaned up. He tells her this, proud of his self-awareness and honesty. She's now twice as mad. She didn't mean it to be a question!

You will need to work hard to find constructive ways to talk directly about the conflict. This will require verbal discipline. A verbally disciplined person is able to say clearly what it was that hurt them and why—but without the sarcasm, sweeping statements, exaggerations, and emotionally charged word choices that pour gasoline on the fire. Verbally disciplined people are mindful of their own relational shortcomings. And so when they speak truth, it is with *grace*.

*A verbally disciplined person is able to say clearly what it was that hurt them and why.*

### For the Purpose of Reconciliation

The last thing Jesus says is truly imperative: We must do all of the above for the purpose of reconciliation, to win back the other person, to restore community. If this is not your motivation, it will corrupt the entire process.

Sometimes the real aim of my confrontation, if I'm truly honest, is not reconciliation. My aim is to inflict pain on the person because I'm so hurt. In this case, direct confrontation will very likely do more damage than good—perhaps even significant emotional damage.

Plainly put, you're not ready for the prior steps until you've dealt honestly with yourself on this step. You may have strong feelings of anger. But is the aim of your heart to work for the best—for yourself, for the other person, for Christ's body? Is your goal the restoration of community as far as it is up to you? If not, you need to do some work in your own heart first.

Pursuing biblical conflict resolution may not always result in the restoration of the relationship. Sometimes separation is needed with the hope that resolve may be possible at a later time. Sometimes you've done all you can and you just have to let it go. But if you have worked through the conflict openly, lovingly, and bravely, you will have satisfaction in your soul. You will have the contentment of knowing that, as far is it was up to you, you pursued peace. You protected that which is precious to God—community (Rom.12:18).

It can be done. You can do it. With God's help, you really can.

A s you worked on the reading, was there a face that kept coming to mind? Is there a conflict that you are avoiding instead of approaching?

If nothing comes to mind, don't force it! Your spiritual exercise this week is to genuinely thank God for the blessings of community you are experiencing right now. As you relate to friends and family this week, thank God for the relational harmony you are enjoying—for past conflicts effectively resolved, for specific events that have deepened your relationships. Make it a week of worship as you reflect on the words, "How good and pleasant it is when brothers dwell together in unity" (Psalm 133:1).

If, on the other hand, a situation *is* readily coming to mind, prayerfully implement what you have read. When you get to the point of going to the other person, consider the following:

- Start by affirming the relationship. ("I'm getting so much joy out of our relationship lately. That's why I want to talk about a pattern that I see developing.")
- Put the conflict in perspective. If it was a fairly small offense—an "ouch"—it can be helpful to say that. ("This is not a big deal. It is more like a ding than a major dent. . . .")
- Next, talk about what happened. ("Often, when we are talking, you cut me off in the middle of my sentences.")
- Express your feelings about what happened. ("That makes me frustrated and a little angry. I feel like my thoughts don't matter to you.")
- Add any observations you have about your own weaknesses in this area. Bring grace to bear. ("I know I sometimes interrupt people too. I don't like when I do that. Maybe that's why it bothers me when you do it.")
- Be clear about what you want from the person. ("I'd like us to really listen to each other and be fully engaged when we're talking.")
- Practice verbal discipline. Avoid sarcasm, cutting remarks, emotionally charged language, sweeping statements. (Don't say things like: "You're always interrupting me. You're a control freak!")

# BIBLE STUDY

We have all learned various ways to handle conflict. If you've not already discovered it, you will soon find that the members of your small group may have very different tendencies when it comes to dealing with relational difficulties. It can help group dynamics—as well as all the other areas of your life—if you are clear about your own patterns.

*We must all learn to manage conflict constructively if we are to live as Christ wants us to.* It is helpful to admit that as we were growing up, few of us had perfect models of conflict resolution. The programming that triggers our reflexes when we enter relational tight spots goes deep in our souls. It is very powerful—and will not change for the better without considerable effort. The beauty of small groups is that they are a place where this effort can be applied and be effective. The work you do in your small group, with the help of the Holy Spirit, will bring great fruit in the development of your ability to live—and to handle conflict—as if Jesus was in your place.

1. Assess your style of managing conflict by using the following scales. Be prepared to explain why you put yourself where you did.

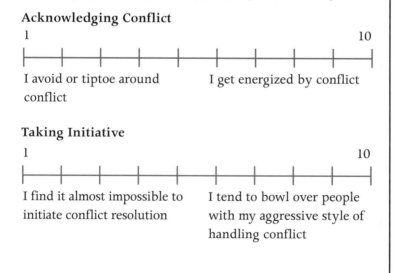

**Acknowledging Conflict**

1                                                                10

I avoid or tiptoe around       I get energized by conflict
conflict

**Taking Initiative**

1                                                                10

I find it almost impossible to   I tend to bowl over people
initiate conflict resolution     with my aggressive style of
                                 handling conflict

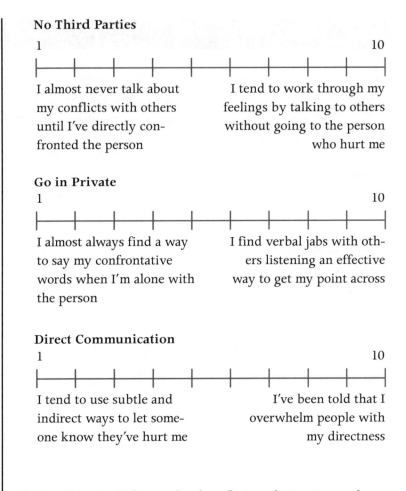

### No Third Parties

1                                                                10

I almost never talk about my conflicts with others until I've directly confronted the person

I tend to work through my feelings by talking to others without going to the person who hurt me

### Go in Private

1                                                                10

I almost always find a way to say my confrontative words when I'm alone with the person

I find verbal jabs with others listening an effective way to get my point across

### Direct Communication

1                                                                10

I tend to use subtle and indirect ways to let someone know they've hurt me

I've been told that I overwhelm people with my directness

2. Describe a typical example of conflict resolution in your home growing up.

How is your style like that now? How is it different?

3. What truths do the following passages from the book of Proverbs express concerning the subject of verbal discipline?

15:1–2

17:27

18:2

18:21

In what ways do you typically need to exercise more verbal discipline when you get frustrated or hurt?

4. Sometimes we fall prey to mistaken or romanticized notions about what community was like in the early church. What insight do the following passages give us about the realities those in the early church faced?

1 Corinthians 1:10–11

1 Corinthians 11:17–18

2 Timothy 2:14–16

5. Paul's instructions in Ephesians 4:22–32 provide a number of useful applications to situations where there is discord. List all the principles that can apply to conflict situations.

NOTE: One important aspect of Paul's instructions, found in Ephesians 4:25, is the command to be angry without sin (that is, to express your anger in nonsinful ways). There are many examples in Paul's life where he was angry with someone. For example, the only mention of "Alexander the coppersmith" is in the context of Paul's anger at him for the harm he did to Paul (2 Tim. 4:14–15). What a way to be immortalized in the pages of Scripture! Yet it shows the honest reaction of Paul being hurt, but trying to be forgiving (see 2 Tim. 4:16). What Paul assumes in this Ephesians passage is that people will get angry, and that anger is not necessarily sinful. One of the hardest areas of conflict to navigate is the emotional side. Paul shows us that we do not need to feel guilty for feeling anger, nor should we tell someone else they have no right to their feelings. What is important is to find ways to honestly express anger without unfairly attacking the other person or doing damage. When we honor each other even in the midst of strong feelings and recognize it's okay to feel what we're feeling (and not condemn another person for what they feel), it can help ease much of the pressure experienced in conflict situations.

6. First Corinthians 13:4–7 is part of Paul's famous "love chapter." We often hear it read at weddings—when love flows naturally. But Paul wrote to a church where love often *didn't* flow naturally. Which aspects of love are you most likely to show in conflict situations? Which are you least likely to show?

7. When we get into conflict, it is the very "nature of the beast" that we become obsessed with our own pain and the injustice done to us. But Scripture repeatedly reminds us that there is something much greater at stake. According to Ephesians 4:1–6 and Jesus' words in John 17:20–23, what is that?

8. In 1 Corinthians 6:1–8, Paul addresses another conflict situation among believers. Describe the situation.

What is Paul's main concern?

Verse 7 poses a tough and very countercultural question. Do you think it's just a rhetorical question? How do you respond to it?

NOTE: In our society, where lawsuits are frequent, Paul's admonishment seems even more countercultural than it did in the first century (although they probably had a hard time swallowing it back then too!). The advice to suffer wrong for the sake of a greater gain really is part of Christian behavior, but it doesn't come easily. The one caution to make here is that some people, by temperament, tend to be nonconfrontive. They justify their lack of initiative with a passage like this. Paul doesn't say Christians should never have conflict or that they should avoid arbitration; he says the fellowship of believers is the place to work it out. When we get stuck—and most of us at some point will—we need to start with godly counsel, not run off to court. That's the way to protect the reputation of Christ's bride, the church, and it ensures that we, as individuals, make progress to live as Jesus would.

9. Think of a situation in which you have recently experienced the breakdown of community. What lessons from this study apply to that situation? What have you learned about yourself? What steps, if any, do you sense the Spirit prompting you to take?

# TAKE-AWAY

*My summary of the main point of this session, and how it impacts me personally:*

NOTE: You will fill in this information after your group discussion. Leave it blank until the conclusion of your meeting.

In the next lesson, the spiritual exercise follows the Bible study and requires setting aside time for reflection. Be sure to allow enough time to thoughtfully engage in it.

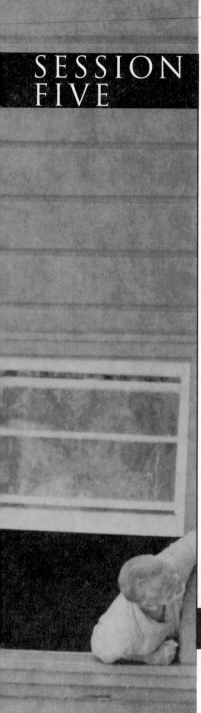

# SESSION
# FIVE

# Forgiveness

Reading adapted from a message by Dr. Lewis B. Smedes

I have bad news and good news. The bad news is that people can hurt you. Sometimes people you trust let you down, betray you, abuse you, and it goes deep. You not only feel hurt, you feel wronged. You didn't deserve it.

You can't forget it. It's like a videotape recorded inside your mind, and there is no on-off button. It comes on randomly. Every time it shows that rerun, you get walloped all over again. There's no delete button. You're stuck with it.

But there is good news. The good news is that God has developed a way to cope with that hurt and to overcome the pain. He invented it. He called it *forgiving* and he invites us to do it with him. There is nothing more important to Jesus than human relationships and nothing more grievous than when a relationship is demolished by someone doing another wrong. It happened to him. He knows. And so he tells us, "Forgive each other." It's the way to bring something good out of a horrible situation.

*He tells us, "Forgive each other." It's the way to bring something good out of a horrible situation.*

## What Do You Do When You Forgive Someone?

It is amazing how difficult a question that is. Did you ever think about it? What do you actually *do* when you forgive someone? I believe that God does three things when he forgives us and when we forgive, we do the same three things.

The first thing you do is rediscover the humanity of the person who hurt you. When somebody hurts me and I'm very wounded and angry, do you know what I do? I reduce that person's humanity to the size of what he did to me. "Fred? Who's Fred? He's the louse who betrayed me." I totally define him in terms of what he did.

When you forgive, you discover that the person who hurt you is a lot more than just what he or she did to you. She is a weak, fragile, sinful human being — not all that different from you.

The Bible gives us a wonderful metaphor for what God does when he forgives. "God washes our sin away." He gets the outer layer of scum and dirt off and says, "Now I can see you for what you really are. What a marvelous creature you are in spite of all your sin." He rediscovers our humanity.

The second thing I think God does is he surrenders his right to get even. He takes this right that we all feel when we've been hurt — the right to balance the score — and he puts it in his hands and looks at it and lets it drop like water, never to be collected again. He gives up his right to get even. So do we when we forgive.

The third thing that happens — and for us, sometimes this takes a while — is that we revise our feelings about the person who did us wrong. Some years ago I taught a class. Sitting toward the front of the room was an extraordinarily lovely woman. At the end of the class, I noticed as she walked out that she was quite visibly handicapped. I met her and asked her to tell me about herself.

She had been an actress living in Beverly Hills — the wife of a star. She got hit by a hit-and-run driver and almost died. She recovered but was handicapped. She went home two weeks later. Her husband took off and left her.

The accident had happened about five years before and I asked her, "Have you forgiven him?"

She said, "I think so."

"What makes you think so?"

*When you forgive, you discover that the person who hurt you is a lot more than just what he or she did to you.*

She said, "I find myself wishing him well."

You know you are in the healing stream of forgiveness when you can get down on your knees—even if you only half mean it—and pray that God would bless the person who hurt you. That is what the grace of God is all about. The Ruler of the universe, the Maker of heaven and earth, *wishes you well*. This is what happens when you forgive someone.

## When Should You Forgive?

My response to this question is: not too late and not too soon. How's that for precise guidance?

*Not too soon*. I worry about "quick-draw" forgivers. Whenever you forgive somebody, you blame them. If you don't blame somebody for something, you don't have to forgive them. Responsibility and blame are always sewed up in the hem of forgiving.

I worry about people who forgive before they have really asked themselves what actually happened. Is that person *truly* to blame? You know, it is possible to forgive people who don't *need* to be forgiven.

Sometimes people forgive fast to avoid the pain. They reason, "If I forgive quickly, I won't experience the pain." You don't forgive to avoid the pain. You forgive to *heal* the pain. And you won't heal the pain unless you have *felt* the pain. Give yourself some time to forgive—not too fast.

But *not too slow*, either. If you wait too long, bitterness and resentment gets woven right into your personality. It becomes part of you. Then trying to get it out is like trying to get a spoonful of ink out of a glass of water.

Here's a key point. Don't wait for the other person to repent or to say, "I'm sorry." Don't wait for a grovel. If you say, "I'll forgive him when he comes on his knees and begs for it," you are taking your happiness and peace and saying, "Here, it's up to you. You decide whether I can ever get free of this pain or not." You're giving the person who clobbered you once the privilege of deciding when you're going to be free and happy again.

*You don't forgive to avoid the pain. You forgive to heal the pain.*

## How Do I Forgive?

This may sound odd, but if need be, begin by pretending. There's a wonderful thing about pretending something. If you pretend it often enough, you become it.

A number of years ago, my younger son got beaten by a cop in front of our house. The neighbors saw everything. I was terribly angry at that cop. My son did not deserve that. I was in a real snit. I told my sister-in-law about it, hoping for a little sympathy. She said, "Why don't you practice what you preach?" That's a lousy thing to tell a preacher when he's hurting!

I had to give a message the next week on the grace of God so I thought, "This has got to be a crash program." I went into my study, got on my knees, and said, "Officer Maloney, in the name of God, I forgive you."

*Creative hypocrisy is when you pretend to be that which you really do want to be.*

I didn't mean a word of it. I said it again and again. I felt like a fool the third time. The thirtieth time the juices began to flow and I began to come to my senses. I realized there may have been a lot more involved in the situation than met the eye. It's hard to be a cop, and he was just trying to do his job. Slowly, I began to rediscover his humanity and surrender my right to get even. I even tried to wish him well.

I call this "creative hypocrisy." Ordinary hypocrisy is when you pretend to be something you have no desire to really be. Creative hypocrisy is when you pretend to be that which you really do *want to be.*

Do it patiently. Forgiveness is a process. Several years after the incident, I heard that the cop had gotten fired. A little voice inside of me said, "Yes! He finally got what he deserved!" Then I thought, "Gee, I must have been kidding myself to think that I had forgiven him." I knew I had backslid, and I had to forgive all over again.

God can forgive in an instant. But we're not God. So be patient. Don't expect every pain to go away immediately and forever. Forgiving is a pilgrimage.

Finally, if forgiveness always comes hard for you, take a journey back into your *own* forgiveness. Reflect on the fact that no matter what you've done in the past, God has forgiven *you*. He has rediscovered the beauty of your humanity. God has surrendered every right to ever get even with you. And *every day* God wishes you well! When you get that sense of forgiveness deep inside of you, it's like a river that washes the anger away. You lose your energy to hate once you know you've been that loved.

When you forgive, you ride the crest of God's great wave of love. When you forgive, you walk hand in hand with God. In the process you set a prisoner free ... and then you discover that the prisoner you set free is *you*.

Adapted from a message by Dr. Lewis B. Smedes. Used with permission.

# BIBLE STUDY

1. How would you rate yourself when it comes to being a forgiving person? On a scale of 1 to 10 (1 being unforgiving and 10 being someone who effortlessly forgives), how do you rate?

1                                                                    10

What factors in your life have influenced this tendency?

2. When you see someone who easily offers forgiveness, what factors do you think make the person that way?

Do you think you've ever offered someone forgiveness too quickly (as suggested in the reading)? Explain.

3. What do you think makes someone unwilling to forgive?

Have you ever withheld forgiveness? What did you want to gain by delaying your forgiveness? What was the result?

4. What should normally happen first, according to Jesus, before we offer forgiveness to someone who has wronged us? (Luke 17:3)

Is it ever permissible to withhold forgiveness if someone doesn't repent? Why or why not?

NOTE: We must make the distinction between *forgiveness* and *reconciliation*. Forgiveness is always possible, because it is in our power to grant. Reconciliation is not always possible, because that requires both parties to agree, which doesn't always happen. Paul's words in Romans are helpful: "If it is possible, as far as it depends on you, live at peace with everyone" (Rom. 12:18). We can and should get to the point where we harbor no unforgiveness; but we cannot always reconcile our differences.

5. Read Jesus' words to Peter in Matthew 18:21–35. According to Jesus, what are the appropriate limits to forgiveness? (vv. 21–22)

How do these words strike you?

NOTE: The rabbinic rule for forgiveness was three times and no more. Peter doubled that, and added one more, surely thinking this quantity showed graciousness sufficient to match God's. (He may have also had in mind Proverbs 24:16, which says a righteous man can fall seven times but get up again.) Jesus is not saying forgiveness is 70 times greater than Peter thought — he's pointing out it's limitless, like the "living water" that continually flows from the heart of a Spirit-born person (John 4:13–14; 7:38). Being forgiving is a way you live, not a commodity parceled out in units.

6. Jesus goes on in Matthew 18:23–35 to tell a parable to explain his extreme statement regarding forgiveness. Outline the facts of the parable below.

NOTE: The ancient Jewish historian Josephus notes that the entire yearly tax imposed on all of Judea, Idumaea, Samaria, Galilee, and Perea combined was 800 talents. It would have taken a common laborer more than nineteen years with no vacations, just to earn one talent. The man in the parable owed 10,000 talents—an enormous sum of money (verse 27 explains it was a loan, so the interest had clearly driven up the amount owed past the initial principle). How relieved he must have felt when he was forgiven! Yet how cruel he was when he confronted the guy who owed him 1/600,000th of the debt he'd been released from!

In verses 32–34 what makes the master's anger burn? What is the main point of the parable?

The reality of forgiveness did *not* make a difference in how the servant who owed 10,000 talents treated others. Why do you suppose it had such little effect on him?

What spiritual reality helps us forgive those who have wronged us?

7. Luke 7:36–50 sheds some additional light on the subject of forgiveness. What is it?

NOTE: Some people misunderstand Jesus' words in Luke 7:47 thinking he is saying the woman's love is the cause of her forgiveness by God. But Jesus is saying her great love is the evidence of it. She was not forgiven because she loved much; she loved much because she was forgiven—her "much love" was the response to forgiveness granted, not its source.

8. Stephen, the first follower of Jesus to be martyred, died at the hands of an angry mob (Acts 7:54–60). What effect might his vision, recorded in verses 55–56, have had on his ability to forgive his murderers?

Stephen's words in verse 60 are reminiscent of Jesus' words on the cross ("Father, forgive them, for they do not know what they are doing" in Luke 23:34). Why would Jesus' example help Stephen forgive his executioners?

9. What is your reaction to the advice from the reading about pretending when you are trying to forgive?

How might Paul's instructions to "live by the Spirit" (Gal. 5:25) and "live by faith, not by sight" (2 Cor. 5:7) be similar to what the reading calls "creative hypocrisy" in the area of offering forgiveness?

When would such "creative hypocrisy" become a farce rather than reality?

10. Second Timothy 4:16 indicates a time when Paul had to practice what he preached. What were the circumstances?

How did he respond?

11. In 1 Timothy 1:12–17, Paul takes a journey back into his own forgiveness. What does he say about his life?

How did this personal awareness impact his own tenderheart-edness and ability to forgive?

12. Now take a journey back into your own forgiveness. Rewrite 1 Timothy 1:12–17, personalizing it. Be specific about your sin and the grace shown you.

# SPIRITUAL EXERCISE

Forgiveness is a process that becomes a way of life. We must remember there are often several steps to forgiveness. We are transformed by moving through the various phases as we're able.

For your exercise this week, set aside a block of time to complete this reflection. You will need unhurried time to ponder what these steps mean for you, and what action you may need to take.

Begin with prayer. Invite God to accompany you in this process.

As you completed this study, did the face of someone who has wronged you come to mind? Is there anyone who provokes a flash of anger when you think of them? Call to mind a family member, coworker, neighbor, roommate, or anyone else who is close enough to you to wound you by their actions.

Be sure to be honest about how you feel—"This person really hurt me." It does no good to minimize what has been done to you, as if it didn't really cause pain (it did), or as if their actions were somehow justified or excusable (they probably weren't).

Now move toward empathy. Imagine this person as a person, not some monster who caused you terrible pain. Can you see their human limitations for what they are? How does God look at the person? The purpose of this is not to excuse any action but to understand the humanity of the one who hurt you.

In "garden-variety" conflicts (in contrast to situations of abuse or trauma), there are usually two sides to the story. That may mean there is a piece of what happened that *you* need to own. It may be small, but it's important you see your own contributions to what happened. What aspect of the situation can you acknowledge as your responsibility?

Finally, consider what you can do to act in loving and forgiving ways. You do not need to feel good, be fully reconciled, or even *like* the person to come up with something that evidences your willingness to give a "blessing instead of a curse."

Remember, forgiveness is a process. You may have to return to this process many times along the way.

One final caveat. Deep hurts, especially from childhood or from sustained physical or emotional abuse, need additional steps in order to heal. What this exercise attempts to cover is the kind of bruising or conflict that is painful but not soul-crushing or life-threatening. If the wounds you suffer are deeper than what is described here, it would probably be a good idea to seek out the help of a Christian counselor who can help you walk through a more comprehensive process.

---

NOTE: For additional help with this exercise, you may want to refer to the following books:

- *God's Outrageous Claims* by Lee Strobel (the chapter entitled "There's Freedom in Forgiving Your Enemies")
- *Forgiving the Dead Man Walking* by Debbie Morris
- *Forgive and Forget* by Lewis Smedes

# TAKE-AWAY

*My summary of the main point of this session, and how it impacts me personally:*

NOTE: You will fill in this information after your group discussion. Leave it blank until the conclusion of your meeting.

# SESSION SIX

BUILDING A PASSIONATELY INCLUSIVE CHURCH

# Building a Passionately Inclusive Church

Reading adapted from a message by Bill Hybels

Just a quick scan of the international scene these days reveals a level of division and murderous hatred rarely witnessed in human history. We have seen horrendous suffering due to ethnic disputes. People are prepared to kill whole groups of people for the "crime" of being different.

A quick scan of our national scene unmasks a level of racial resentment and division that ought to make all of us wake up and smell the coffee. Even if people don't act on every impulse, the tensions beneath the surface are always there, and frequently make the evening news.

A bit closer to home, I've been thinking a lot about the condition of churches around the country. The ten o'clock Sunday morning hour is the most segregated hour in America's week. That is very sad. And going beyond that, while millions of openhearted spiritual seekers are just waiting to be invited and enfolded into the community of the local church, many churches really don't seem to care that much. They are talking about peripheral matters instead of grace. They are not challenging and commissioning their members to open their arms to people beyond their walls. Instead, there are the subtle signals given as to who is welcome and who isn't, who has their act together enough to come in and who doesn't.

Sometimes when I think about the hatred, the divisions, the apathy, I feel overwhelmed. I wonder if there is

*Sometimes when I think about the hatred, the divisions, the apathy, I feel overwhelmed. I wonder if there is any hope for a change.*

*any* hope for a change. But then something deep within me whispers, "God can change the composition of a human heart." He can. God can transform a hateful heart into a loving heart. God can transform an apathetic heart into a strongly caring heart. God can bring passionate inclusivity into a heart that has only known passionate exclusivity. But I have a distinct feeling that only God can.

## Is There a Blockage in Your Heart?

How is your heart today? What is going on inside of it? How open is it to people of different races? How open is it to people of higher or lower educational or economic status than you? How open is your heart to people who differ with you politically? How open is your heart to people who are far from God? You know the type—profane, immoral people.

*If you look closely at your heart, you might find that you have some heart disease.*

If you look closely at your heart, you might find that you have some heart disease. You might find that there's some blockage—a restricted flow of grace where love should be coursing through your veins.

One day, Jesus was surrounded by a crowd of spiritual castaways—scoundrels, really. They were the kind of people who make the most upstanding church people bristle. They had the kind of morals and vocabulary that was just not acceptable. But they were listening to Jesus with riveted attention.

While Jesus was talking with this crowd, the religious leaders of that day took note of Jesus' interaction with these people and they began murmuring among themselves. Someone of Jesus' stature should not be so careless about the company he keeps. Surely, he should show more discernment.

Surely, there are some people who should be included and some who ought to be excluded. There are some who should sit in the front of the bus, and there are some who should sit in the back. There are those with accents, and those who speak properly, like me. There are those so incredibly stupid that they vote the wrong side of every political issue, and then there are people like me who get it right every time.

The Pharisees thought they had it all figured out. They knew who mattered and who didn't.

But before we judge the Pharisees too harshly, it is my long-held belief that every human being carries in his or her heart an unpublished, but quite conscious, list of who has value in this world and who doesn't. It is a part of our shadowy side. It is a reflection of our fallenness — a manifestation of the evil at work within us.

I'm ashamed to admit it, but I have a list. I have tried for twenty-five years to shrink the list. I'd love to say that my list is all gone. But still sometimes, in unguarded moments, when I least expect it, my heart turns cold toward certain kinds of people. I find myself freezing them out and keeping them away and setting them aside and excluding them.

*Every human being carries in his or her heart an unpublished, but quite conscious, list of who has value in this world and who doesn't.*

I let them know in certain ways that I have no interest whatsoever in being in community with them. I don't want to know and be known by them. I don't want to love and be loved by them. I don't want to serve and be served, celebrate and be celebrated by them. I just don't. Even worse, I lose clarity on how God feels about them.

The truth is, you have a list, too. Don't say you don't. We all have a list. Part of growing as a spiritual person is to stop denying that our list exists. We need to become ruthlessly aware of it. Most of all, we need to ask God to do the kind of heart surgery that only he can do.

### Pursuing Passionate Inclusivity

As you sit reading these words, whether you are rich or poor, black or white, whether you are male or female, young or old, educated or uneducated, scarred or squeaky clean or anything in between, you are more precious to God than you could ever imagine. Your being in community with him is such a big deal that he took the most extreme measure he could take. When his arms were extended and nailed on the crossbar they were extended to you—simply because he wanted *you* included. And he did it without batting an eye, because you matter to him.

The reality of that truth always has a way of melting the hardness and exclusivity of my heart. When I realize how much I matter to God, then I start looking around at other people and I think, "Well, then he matters to God, too . . . and she matters to God . . . and he matters to God." I start realizing that every person I interact with today, or tomorrow, or every day for the rest of my life is someone for whom Christ died. If they matter that much to him, they ought to matter to me. My arms should be open wider. I should be passionately inclusive of every breathing human being.

When I let these kinds of thoughts seep into my spirit and become the prevalent thoughts in my mind, I begin to feel a bigger heart toward people. I look at them differently. I care about them more. I long for them to come to Christ and then come into community in a little group in a church where they can be known, loved, served, and celebrated. It's the strangest thing to feel your heart get bigger.

What would happen if all of us got honest about our lists. What would happen if all of us got serious in praying, "God, increase my ability to love; enlarge my capacity to include; grow my desire to extend Your community to a wider and wider circle of people"?

I think God would respond . . . and transform. I think he would soften our hearts and open them wider.

May we commit together to making that choice—to becoming radically inclusive people, in radically inclusive community that passionately reflects the heart of our radically inclusive God.

*I should be passionately inclusive of every breathing human being.*

# SPIRITUAL EXERCISE

Your challenge this week is to live with this prayer:

*Lord, increase my ability to love, and enlarge my capacity to include.*

Consider writing the prayer on a card and posting it on your dashboard, your mirror, or your desk. Then, as you go through your day—at work, in the neighborhood, in the store, at church—try to become aware of your own personal list. What kind of person do you tend to avoid or feel cool toward? What factors tend to make you want to exclude instead of include? Ethnic background? Economic class? Gender difference? Political views? Body shape?

As you pray the above prayer through these encounters, what difference, if any, does it make on your desire to extend Christ and his community? What realistic steps could you take to begin breaking through these barriers?

1. Think back to a time when you were excluded by someone (or a group of people). It may have been recently or a long time ago. Describe that situation, noting why you were left out:

   What did you feel like when that happened?

   What was the impact of that experience on you (short-term and long-term)?

   From your experience, how important is a feeling of belonging?

2. In your family growing up, were certain kinds of people "on the outside" — on an unwritten list of those who don't have as much value as the rest of us?

Why do you think people get put on such a list?

How do you still struggle with an internal list of people who are "less than"?

3. Read Ephesians 2:1–5, 12–13, and 19. Contrast all of what *was* true about you with what is *now* true because of Christ.

God could have left you on the outside—there is no logical or compelling reason he *had* to offer you new life or a place of belonging in his family. However, he didn't leave you adrift. Paul stresses that God chose to include you, to reach out to make a place for you in his kingdom. What was your worthiness for such acceptance, according to these verses?

What, according to Paul, motivated God to want to include all of us? (Eph. 2:4, 7)

4. What would be true for you today if God had *not* been an inclusive God—how would your life be different?

5. In spite of his close association to Jesus, Peter the apostle had a list of those who were "unclean" (Acts 10:28). How did God get him to move past his prejudices? (Acts 11:1–18)

What lesson was engraved on Peter's heart through this experience? (Acts 10:34–35; 11:9, 17, 18)

6. Every day, we have the choice to be exclusive and not care about those outside the faith, or to be inclusive and work to invite others into the family of God. For Paul, he couldn't help but devote his whole life to reaching out—as he himself had been reached out to (Eph. 3:7–9). Which of the following tend to keep you from being more passionately inclusive? Explain each one you identify with:

• Low passion in my own walk with God

• Feel comfortable with the way things are

• Fear of jeopardizing the good fellowship I've found by allowing others in

• Our church is already so big—who needs even more people?

• Certain kinds of people make me uncomfortable

• Other:

7. Paul wanted the churches he led to be free from any kind of exclusivity. What are common categories that separated people in his day which being in Christ has transcended? (Gal. 3:28)

What are some similar categories in our day?

What can be done to prevent the message of Christ from being distorted by such distinctions both in your life and in the life of the church?

8. Consider your own struggles with various forms of exclusivity.

Rate yourself on the following scale. Be prepared to discuss why you put yourself where you did.

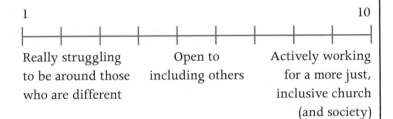

1                                                                10
Really struggling          Open to              Actively working
to be around those    including others          for a more just,
who are different                                inclusive church
                                                   (and society)

What would help you to take the next step?

9. Now take some time to prayerfully and thoughtfully respond to the following:

   *Lord, I want to thank you for including me, especially because . . .*

   *Lord, I need your help to overcome my lack of inclusivity, especially concerning . . .*

*Father, what can I do to increase my ability to love? To enlarge my capacity to include? (Write down any impressions you get.)*

*What is a way this week I could extend community or salvation to someone currently on the outside? (Again, write down any ideas you get.)*

# TAKE-AWAY

*My summary of the main point of this session, and how it impacts me personally:*

NOTE: You will fill in this information after your group discussion. Leave it blank until the conclusion of your meeting.

# SESSION
# SEVEN

## BEING "FOR"
## ONE ANOTHER

# Being "For" One Another

Reading adapted from a message by John Ortberg

Her name was Pandy. She had lost a good deal of her hair, one of her arms was missing, and generally speaking, she'd had the stuffing knocked out of her. She was my sister Barbie's favorite doll.

She hadn't always looked like this. She had been a personally selected Christmas gift by a cherished aunt who had traveled to Marshall Field's in faraway Chicago to find her. Her face and hands were made of rubber so that they looked real, but her body was stuffed with rags to feel soft and squeezable, like a real baby.

When Pandy was young and a looker, Barbie loved her. She loved her with a love that was too strong for Pandy's own good. Barbie slept with Pandy next to her and ate with Pandy beside her. When Barbie could get away with it, Pandy took a bath with her. For Pandy, it was a nearly fatal attraction.

By the time I knew Pandy, she was a mess. She was no longer a valuable doll. I'm not sure we could have given her away. But for reasons no one could quite figure out, my sister loved that little rag doll still. She loved her as strongly in the days of her raggedness as she ever had in her days of great beauty. Barbie loved that little doll with the kind of love that made the doll precious to anyone who loved Barbie. To love Barbie was to love Pandy. It was a package deal.

Two things are true about us. First, *we are all rag dolls.* Flawed and wounded, broken and bent. Partly, our

*We are all rag dolls.*

raggedness is something that happens *to* us. Our genes set us up for certain weaknesses. Our loved ones let us down when we need them most. But that's not the whole story. We each make our own deposits into the ragged account of the human race. We choose to deceive when the truth begs to be spoken. We grumble when generous praise is called for. We betray when we are bound by oaths of loyalty. Raggedness permeates our whole being. We are rag dolls, all right.

But the second truth is that *we are God's rag dolls*. He knows about our raggedness and loves us anyway. Paul put it like this: "For while we were still weak, at the right time, Christ died for the ungodly. . . . God proves his love for us in that while we were still sinners Christ died for us" (Rom. 5:6, 8 NRSV). God is fully aware of our secret. He knows we are rag dolls. But God has gone to the ultimate length to prove his love for us. He died at the *right time*—when we were ragged, weak, sinful— to make us new. This is a love beyond reason. This is the love of God.

*To be* for *someone means that I am in their corner.*

There are two commands that form the heart of our response to God's love, and they cannot be separated. All of God's will comes down to this: Love the Lord your God with all your heart, soul, mind, and strength; and love your neighbor as yourself. "Love me, love my rag dolls," God says. It's a package deal.

If we are serious about loving God, we must be serious about loving the people around us. But how is this love expressed? There are many ways, to be sure. But somewhere very close to the core is this: Love is being *for* the one who is loved.

## Balcony People

If I love someone, I long for them to flourish and blossom. I want them to realize all their potential. To be *for* someone means that I am in their corner. I am cheering them on. I am a voice of encouragement.

Encouragement. In Greek, the word is *paraklesis*. It is used more than one hundred times in the New Testament, so its importance can't be missed. Its very origin creates a picture, "to be called alongside of." Gregory of Nyssa, an early church father, expressed it this way:

> At horse races the spectators intent on victory shout to their favorites in the contest.... From the stands they participate in the race with their eyes, thinking to incite the charioteer to keener effort, at the same time urging the horses on while leaning forward and flailing the air with their outstretched hands instead of a whip.

> ... I seem to be doing the same thing myself, most valued friend and brother. While you are competing admirably in the divine race along the course of virtue ... I exhort, urge, and encourage you vigorously to increase your speed.

Balcony people are those who take their place in the stands urging, exhorting, and encouraging, while you run the race of your life. The New Testament writers consistently urge us to become balcony people for one another.

> *Balcony people are those who take their place in the stands urging, exhorting, and encouraging, while you run the race of your life.*

> Therefore encourage [parakaleite] one another and build each other up, just as in fact you are doing.
> —1 Thessalonians 5:11

> And let us consider how we may spur one another on toward love and good deeds. Let us not give up meeting together, as some are in the habit of doing, but let us encourage [parakalountes] one another ...
> —Hebrews 10:24–25

> ... I have written to you briefly, encouraging [parakalon] you...
> —1 Peter 5:12

Encouragement, properly understood, is essential language in the new community.

## Community Killers

Being *for* someone means I celebrate their victories and mourn their setbacks. It means I deeply and sincerely wish them well.

This is not easy to do. It doesn't take much truth-telling for me to admit that I don't want my enemies to succeed. More humbling is the fact that, deep down, I often don't even want my friends to succeed too much.

One of my earliest church memories is of a time when our Sunday School teacher decided to have a Bible verse memorizing contest. We all had a poster that went on the wall, and for every verse you could recite, you'd get a sticker. If you won the contest, you would win a white Bible with your name printed on it in gold letters. I wanted that Bible so badly I would have violated most of what's in it to get hold of it.

*Competition, comparison, envy—they are all anticommunity.*

Not long into the contest it became clear that the competition was really between me and a girl named Louise—a freckle-faced, snotty little kid with big glasses. For weeks it was nip and tuck between the two of us. We matched each other sticker for sticker. But in the final month she began to pull away. In the final week, it was clear she was going to win.

I wanted the Bible so much that I began to wonder what I could do about Louise. So I killed her. At least in my mind I did. I did not like her. I did not rejoice when her name was the one called. I did not celebrate her victory.

I hate to say it, but that was not the last time that I've turned church into a contest.

Competition, comparison, envy—they are all anti-community. Paul said that we are to "rejoice with those who rejoice; [and] mourn with those who mourn" (Rom. 12:15). Competition and envy cause me to mourn when others *rejoice* and rejoice when others *mourn*. They lead me to diminish others instead of building them up. They cause me to be *opposed* to other people instead of being *for* them.

## Being "For" Is Not Being "Soft"

Love is often confused with softness. When we speak of doing "the loving thing," we sometimes think it means "always doing what the person I love would want me to do." This is, of course, not love; it is not even sane. Try it with a three-year-old and odds are he'll never make it to four.

Being *for* someone is deeper than just wanting to spare them pain. If I am really *for* a person, I am willing to risk saying painful things, if pain is the only way to bring growth. For "the Lord disciplines those He loves" (Heb. 12:6). True love is ready to warn, reprove, confront, or admonish when it is needed. But only humbly, reluctantly.

True love never desires to inflict pain for pain's sake. All too often, I'm not only willing to inflict pain on someone, I'm looking forward to it. Probably a safe guideline is that I need to be very careful of creating pain for another person if I feel a twinge of enjoyment in the process.

## God Is *For* You

"If God is for us, who can be against us? . . . Who shall separate us from the love of Christ?" (Rom. 8:31, 35) This is the truth that staggered the apostle Paul. For all of his raggedness, *God* was *for* him.

And the God of the universe is *for* you. He longs for you to blossom and flourish. He celebrates your victories. He mourns your setbacks. He is on your side. He is in the balcony, cheering you on.

*If I am really* for *a person, I am willing to risk saying painful things, if pain is the only way to bring growth.*

# SPIRITUAL EXERCISE

This week, experiment with the radical commitment of being *for* the people in your relational world. Throughout your daily encounters, ask yourself the question, "How can I be a 'balcony person' right now?" For example:

- How could you build up someone who you often tend to over-look completely—a waitress, busboy, cashier, etc.? Consider looking them in the eye, saying a sincere "thank-you," extending a simple compliment, even leaving a more generous tip! How creative can you be in conveying the message that they matter to a God who is *for* them?
- Be especially generous with encouragement this week. When you notice something worthy of affirmation, don't hold back. *When you see it, say it!* Err on the side of overdoing it a bit.
- Deliberately try building up someone who is a difficult person in your life. Stretch yourself to be *for* them in some way this week. See what happens, positive or negative.
- Notice when someone is succeeding, and celebrate it. Find the people who are winning at their game and cheer them on. Do this even if (*especially* if) it means breaking through your own feelings of competitiveness or envy. (Maybe even go out on a limb and talk to them about those feelings!)
- Encouraging someone might mean lovingly expressing a concern regarding a pattern of behavior. You might want to say, "I am *for* you. I care about you, that's why I'm saying this." Let them know that you're on their side.
- Be *for* someone this week through concentrated prayer. If appropriate, send them a note letting them know you are praying on their behalf.
- Finally, make a point this week of encouraging the individual members of your small group. On a separate piece of paper, complete the following thought regarding each person in the group: One thing I really appreciate about you is . . .

Bring these encouragement statements with you to your next small group meeting (or retreat, if your group chooses that option).

1. Think back on a time in your life when someone was really *for* you. What concrete actions on their part made you feel that way? Be as specific as you can.

   What impact did that have?

2. A wise theologian was asked to summarize the gospel in just one sentence. Pausing for only a moment, he chose one single phrase—*God is for us!* Romans 8 is the pinnacle of Paul's teaching on God being *for* us. Read through the entire chapter. Then note below all of the diverse ways that God is *for* those who have trusted Christ.

In what ways have you felt God being *for* you in any of these specific ways in recent months?

---

NOTE: One way we communicate being for someone is empathizing with them—seeking to enter into their joy or sorrow. In Romans 8, Paul makes one of the most staggering claims in the Bible, that God actually took on "the likeness of sinful flesh" (v. 3 NRSV). In other words, Jesus really experienced the temptations and frustrations that all human beings do—only without sinning. You will never have someone empathize with you the way God can.

---

3. Romans 8:31–39 has been called by one great theologian a statement of "truly reverent defiance." In a way, each of us needs to bring an attitude of "truly reverent defiance" against anything that would diminish our personal confidence in God's being *for* us. For example:

A false sense of guilt or inadequacy

Failure

Human opposition

Disapproval from others

Suffering

All these must be ruthlessly countered by a sanctified spirit of defiance that insists on clinging to the unyielding promises of God. What tempts you to feel distant or separated from God? Where do you especially need "truly reverent defiance" these days?

4. In Romans 8:33–34, Paul is using the picture of a courtroom. In U.S. law there is a tradition that once a person has been tried and found innocent they cannot be accused and retried—no possibility of "double jeopardy." Paul says that God himself has tried us. His throne is the Supreme Court and God has declared us innocent, loved, and free in Christ. There is simply no power able to overturn that verdict—no "spiritual double jeopardy." The trial's over. The verdict's in. You're free.

How might it affect your prayer life and your confidence with God if you were to live in full assurance of God's final verdict of "innocent" for your life?

5. There is a strong temptation to judge the extent to which you feel God is *for* you by how smoothly your life is going at any particular time. How tempted are you to do that?

How smoothly was Paul's life going at the time? (see 2 Cor. 11:24–29)

What do you think enabled Paul to make the bold statement that he did in Romans 8:28?

Paul *really believed* that God was *for* him, even in the worst of times. It wasn't just head knowledge or theological truth. It was a belief that shaped the way Paul did life. How would your life be different if you *really* believed that God was *for* you through all of life's circumstances? What effect would it have on your confidence, anxiety level, and attitudes?

6. Paul never kept for himself what he received from God. Whatever he received "vertically" (from God) found expression "horizontally" in community. How does Paul urge us to be *for* each other?

Galatians 5:13−14

Romans 12:9−11

1 Thessalonians 5:11

7. Encouragement has many faces in the New Testament. Consider the following forms that encouragement takes:

*To believe in someone, to see their giftedness and ability to contribute.* (1 Tim. 4:12−15; 2 Tim. 1:6−7)

The last time someone encouraged me this way was:

*To exhort someone, to build their character by confronting them even when it may involve saying hard things.* (2 Tim. 4:2; 2 Thess. 3:11−13)

The last time someone encouraged me this way was:

*To comfort, console, give courage to.* (2 Cor. 1:3−6; 2 Thess. 2:16)

The last time someone encouraged me this way was:

*To challenge, to urge, to entreat one to greater heights, deeper growth.* (Eph. 4:1 [The use of *parakalo* in this verse conveys the sense, "*I dare you* to . . ."])

The last time someone encouraged me this way was:

*To express support and affirmation through tangible gifts.* (Acts 4:36–37 [Originally called Joseph, he received a new name from the apostles: Barnabas—*Uios Parakleseos*—"son of encouragement."]; 2 Cor. 8:1–7)

The last time someone encouraged me this way was:

8. How is your walk with Christ different today because someone took the time to encourage you in the above ways? In what ways were those acts of encouragement spiritually transforming?

9. How much of an encourager are *you* these days? Would your name have appeared above if a close friend or family member was answering question 7?

10. What most often hinders you from being an encourager?

_____Encouragement just doesn't come naturally for me

_____I'm usually so hurried I don't stop to do it

_____I admit that competition and envy often get in the way

_____Just plain, old self-centeredness

_____Other:

11. What is one way in which you would like to feel the encouragement of others in your group?

What is one way that you would like to grow in expressing encouragement to others in your group?

NOTE: As important as encouragement is, it, like anything else, can be misused. This is particularly true when it comes to cross-gender relationships where encouraging words can lead to the inappropriate expression of affection.

As always, we need to look to Jesus' model. He never avoided cross-gender relationships. He had rich relationships with women followers. But his interactions were always characterized by wisdom and purity. A few simple questions can help us ensure that our interactions are purely and wisely centered:

1. Is this an interaction I'd have with a brother or sister? (see 1 Timothy 5:1–2)
2. (If married) Would my spouse be comfortable with my words or actions in this setting?
3. If this interaction were videotaped and made public, would I feel embarrassed?

If there are men and women in your small group, hopefully you are experiencing rich times of fellowship as brothers and sisters in Christ. That is a gift worth cherishing and protecting. With care, discernment, and accountability, you can keep enjoying these kind of relationships without violating healthy boundaries.

# TAKE-AWAY

*My summary of the main point of this session, and how it impacts me personally:*

> NOTE: You will fill in this information after your group discussion. Leave it blank until the conclusion of your meeting.

# SOLITUDE WORKSHEET

## For Optional Retreat

### Acknowledge God's Presence

Begin by acknowledging God is with you. Invite him to be real to you in your experience right now. Welcome him into the world of your thoughts and recognize that he is more familiar with your inner workings than even you are.

### Still Yourself

It's common when entering solitude to have your thoughts "jump around like monkeys in a banana tree" (to quote one writer's description). Are you worried about something or thinking of some task you have to do? Whatever might be grabbing your attention, lift these concerns to God. If it would be helpful, write those thoughts down so you can address them later. When you feel like you've presented them to him and you've let them go — as best you can for now — move on to the main part of this solitude exercise: "Interacting with God."

### Interacting with God

Read Romans 8 slowly. Don't read this chapter like you would skim the newspaper — read it the way you would pore over every word of a love letter, looking intently for what each phrase might mean.

Go back through the chapter and be aware of any phrase or word which touches you at a deep level. Create a place in your heart to hear these words as God's message to you. Write down those phrases that impact you, or perhaps even rewrite parts of the passage in your own words.

What do you want to say to God in response to these truths? If you find your heart touched, talk to God about that. Or maybe it feels like nothing significant is happening. Talk to him about that too. Tell him freely what you're feeling — hope, joy, dryness, longing . . . whatever. Make this a time of true conversation, where you both speak and listen.

## Conclusion

When your time is almost up, conclude by thanking God for his promise that he is *for* you and there is no end to his love for you.

---

NOTE: Before you return to the group, take a few minutes to think about the different people in your small group. Take out your encouragement messages to each person you prepared before the retreat. As you look over what you wrote in the blank "One thing I really appreciate about you is . . . ," can you think of any additional thoughts you'd like to add? Don't worry if nothing comes to mind, but if it does, be sure to add it to the note.

---

# Leader's Guide

## How to Use This Discussion Guide

### Doers of the Word

One of the reasons small groups are so effective is because when people are face-to-face, they can discuss and process information instead of merely listening passively. *God's truths are transforming* only to the extent they are received and absorbed. Just as uneaten food cannot nourish, truth "out there"—either in a book or spoken by a teacher—cannot make a difference if it is undigested. Even if it is bitten off and chewed, it must be swallowed and made part of each cell to truly give life.

The spiritual transformation at the heart of this Bible study series can occur only if people get truth and make that truth part of their lives. Reading about sit-ups leaves you flabby; doing sit-ups gives you strong abdominals. That's why in every session, we present group members with exercises to do during the week. They also study Scripture on their own in (hopefully) unhurried settings where they can meditate on and ponder the truths that are encountered. Group discussion is the other way we've designed for them to grab hold of these important lessons.

This study is not a correspondence course. It's a personal and group experience designed to help believers find a biblical approach to their spiritual lives that really works. We recognize that people have a variety of learning styles, so we've tried to incorporate a variety of ways to learn. One of the most important ways they will learn is when they meet together to process the information verbally in a group.

### Not Question-by-Question

One approach to learning used by some small groups encourages members to systematically discuss *everything* they learn on their own during the group time. Such material is designed so group members do a study and then report what their answers were for each question. While this approach is thorough, it can become boring. The method we've adopted includes individual study, but we do not suggest discussing *everything* in the session when you meet. Instead, questions are given to leaders (hence, this Leader's Guide) to get at the heart of the material without being rote recitations of the answers the members came up with on their own. This may be a bit confusing at first, because some people fill in the blanks, expecting each answer to be discussed, and discussed in the order they wrote them down. Instead, you, as a leader, will be asking questions *based* on their study, but not necessarily numerically corresponding to their study. We think this technique of handling the sessions has the best of both approaches: individual learning is reinforced in the group setting without becoming wearisome.

It is also important that you understand you will not be able to cover all the material provided each week. We give you more than you can use in every session—not to frustrate you, but to give you enough so you can pick and choose. *Base your session plan on the needs of individual members of your group.*

There may be a few times when the material is so relevant to your group members that every question seems to fit. Don't feel bad about taking two weeks on a session. The purpose of this series is transformational life-change, not timely book completion!

For the final session, we've actually given you an overnight retreat option so that you can process the material in a thorough manner and leisurely engage in a group encouragment experience.

### Getting Ready for *Your* Group

We suggest that to prepare for a meeting, you first do the study yourself and spend some time doing the spiritual exercise. Then look over the questions we've given you in the Leader's Guide. As you consider your group members and the amount of discussion time you have, ask yourself if the questions listed for that session relate to your group's needs. Would some other questions fit better? We've tried to highlight the main points of each session, but you may feel you need to hit some aspect harder than we did, or not spend as much time on a point. As long as your preparation is based on knowledge of your group, customize the session however you see fit.

As we pointed out, you may have to adapt the material because of time considerations. It is very hard to discuss every topic in a given session in detail—we certainly don't recommend it. You may also only have a limited time because of the nature of your group. Again, the purpose isn't to cover every question exhaustively, but to get the main point across in each session (whatever incidental discussion may otherwise occur). As a guide to your preparation, review the *Primary Focus* statement at the beginning and the *Session Highlights* paragraph at the end of each session's Leader's Guide. They represent our attempt to summarize what we were trying to get across in writing the sessions. If your questions get at those points, you're on the right track.

### A Guide, Not a Guru

Now a word about your role as leader. We believe all small groups need a leader. While it is easy to see that a group discussion would get off track without a facilitator, we would like you to ponder another very important reason you hold the position you do.

This Bible study series is about spiritual growth—about Christ being formed in each of us. One of the greatest gifts you can give another person is to pay attention to his or her spiritual life. As a leader, you will serve your group members by observing their lives and trying to hear, in the questions they ask and the answers they give, where they are in their spiritual development. Your discerning observations are an invaluable contribution to their spiritual progress. That attention, prayer, and insight is an extremely rare gift—but it is revolutionary for those blessed enough to have such a person in their lives. You are that person. You give that gift. You can bring that blessing.

People desperately need clarity about spirituality. Someone needs to blow away the fog that surrounds the concept of what it means to live a spiritual life and give believers concrete ideas how to pursue it. Spiritual life is just *life*. It's that simple. Christ-followers must invite God into all aspects of life, even the everyday routines. That is where we spend most of our time anyway, so that is where we must be with God. If not, the Christian life will become pretense, or hypocrisy. We must decompartmentalize life so that we share it all with God in a barrier-free union with him.

We say all this so that you, the leader, can be encouraged in and focused on your role. You are the person observing how people are doing. You are the one who detects the doors people will not let God through, the one who sees the blind spots they don't, the one who gently points out the unending patience of God who will not stop working in us until "his work is completed" (Phil. 1:6). You will hold many secret conversations with God about the people in your group—while you meet, during a phone call, sitting across the table at lunch, when you're alone. In addition to making the meeting happen, this is one of the most important things you can do to be a catalyst for life-change. That is why you're meeting together anyway—to see people become more like Christ. If you lead as a *facilitator* of discussion, not a teacher, and a *listener* rather than the one who should be listened to, you will see great changes in the members of your group.

# SESSION ONE

## *This Is a Friendship*

**Primary Focus:** To learn fundamental realities about building friendships.

*Remember that these questions do not correspond numerically with the questions in the assignment. We do not recommend simply going over what your group members put for their answers—that will probably result in a tedious discussion at best. Rather, use some or all of these questions (and perhaps some of your own) to stimulate discussion; that way, you'll be processing the content of the session from a fresh perspective each meeting.*

1. What was it like this week noticing how Jesus is your friend? When did that seem most true? When was that hard? In what ways do you see your relationship with God impacting your human relationships?

2. How did you react to the part of the reading about realistic expectations for relationships? Do you tend to be more idealistic or more pessimistic about the possibility of good relationships?

3. *(Regarding question 7 in the Bible study)* To which aspects of Paul's love of community did you relate? Which seemed more foreign to you?

4. Describe a defining moment or era in your life with respect to your pursuit of Christian community.

5. *(Regarding question 10 in the Bible study)* How did you answer this question concerning your present "want to" factor?

6. *(Regarding question 12 in the Bible study)* Explain your answer to the last continuum.

7. *(Regarding question 13 in the Bible study)* What goals for our small group would you like to see accomplished in this series of sessions?

NOTE: It might be a good idea to compile this list from everybody's answers and form a "group covenant" for this study. It is always a good idea for groups to have some sort of contract—an understanding of expectations mutually agreed upon. If you don't have such a covenant, you may want to make one; at a minimum, it would be good to set expectations for these next several weeks. Note that people also often have very idealistic goals, and a dose of realism is in order. You as the leader are not a bad leader if everybody's expectations are not met—that's just not possible (see the note after Bible study question 12). But the more people get their hopes and dreams out on the table, the better the possibility some of them will be realized.

**Take-Away:** At the conclusion of your discussion each week, take a few minutes to have group members sum up the session and its impact on them by filling in the Take-Away section at the end of each session. Don't tell them what they are supposed to write—let them be true to their own experiences. When they have written their summaries, have everyone share with the others what they wrote. Statements should be similar to the statements in Session Highlights. If you feel the whole group may have missed an important aspect of the session, be sure to bring that up in the closing discussion.

**Session Highlights**: Community is fundamental to spiritual life; relationships must be wanted and cultivated; we must intentionally work at asking deeper questions to make relationships grow; security in our relationship with God helps us take risks in relationships with people.

NOTE: As part of this study guide, we've included a group retreat as part of Session 7. We encourage you as the leader to make the plans necessary to take this retreat with your group when you get to that session. (The retreat will replace your normal group meeting.) Set aside the dates enough in advance to ensure people will attend. Several of the sessions in this study may take more than one meeting to complete, so keep that in mind and schedule accordingly. This retreat could be the highlight of your time together, so do all you can to try to make it a reality.

## Love Pays Attention

**Primary Focus:** Paying attention is one of the most powerful ways to express love.

1. How did the spiritual exercise go this week? How easy was it for you to be fully present when others were speaking? How hard was it to stay focused on the other person instead of bringing the conversation around to yourself? What did you learn through this exercise?

2. As you tried to listen to others with a "third ear"—one attuned to the Holy Spirit—was there anything you sensed God saying to you, through them or to them through you?

3. Have you ever had someone notice something about you that was especially significant to you? From your experience, what is the connection between being noticed and feeling loved?

4. *(Regarding questions 1 and 2 in the Bible study)* What stood out most concerning God's attentiveness?

5. *(Regarding question 3 in the Bible study)* Is there any time recently when you have strongly felt the attentiveness of God toward you—a time when he was particularly mindful of some detail in your life? What impact did that experience have on you?

6. *(Regarding question 4 in the Bible study)* How about a time when you felt just the opposite—when you couldn't feel God's presence or attention? What, in your own spiritual development, has helped you trust even in the midst of times like these?

7. *(Regarding question 5 in the Bible study)* How do you rate your attentiveness toward God these days? How well are you noticing, remembering, listening to him?

8. Is there a particular relationship where it is consistently difficult for you to "attend"? What do you think contributes to that? Do you sense the Spirit prompting you in any way?

9. *(Regarding question 9 in the Bible study)* How are we doing as a group when it comes to paying attention to each other?

**Session Highlights:** One of the most powerful ways to express love to another person is by paying attention—noticing, remembering, listening; God consistently "turns his face" toward us with loving attention to the details of our lives; if we are to live as Jesus would if he were in our place, we must learn to live this out in our relationships.

## *Knowing and Being Known*

**Primary Focus:** To learn the value of progressing steadily into more authentic relationships.

---

NOTE: The first eight questions cover the content presented in the session and your group members' reflections based on the Bible study. The last question is designed to actually further the goal of "knowing and being known." Obviously, this time of sharing should not be rushed. As always, if you think you will be pressed for time, consider taking two group meetings—or more if the conversations are rich—to handle this material. Even then, you may need to be selective as to which of the following questions (or others of your own creation) you choose to explore.

---

1. The reading mentioned a man whose friend was getting to know his "human side." How easily do people see *your* human side? Do you think people want to know you as you really are, or do you think they prefer a modified version? Why?

2. Why do you think in church—of all places—people are more apt to hide and project a more "acceptable" image of themselves?

3. Of the four different relational environments described by the circles, which come most naturally for you? Which is the one you think you most need to work on?

4. (*Regarding question 1 in the Bible study*) What did you think Bonhoeffer meant by "Let him who cannot be alone beware of community"?

5. What did you observe about your own tendencies to hide sinful or undesirable aspects of who you are from God?

6. Describe a time when you were sharpened spiritually because someone in this group took a risk and shared a struggle, weakness, or point of pain.

7. (*Regarding question 11 in the Bible study*) What role do you think others play in diagnosing our spiritual growth points? What role do they play in our actual transformation?

8. Describe in one sentence the way large group teaching and worship services have impacted your spiritual transformation this year.

9. Respond to one of the following questions from question 12 in the Bible study. (Feel free to do all three if time permits.)

   What is one thing that a lot of people assume about you that you honestly wish they wouldn't?

   What is one of your greatest personal desires for the year?

   What is one of your greatest fears for the year?

NOTE: Be patient as people take steps toward becoming more open and vulnerable. Encourage, but don't harass people—for many, opening up is extremely hard and goes against long-established, ingrained patterns. Your example will always be the best motivation. Gently pull, don't push, in this area, and recognize this group experience is only one of many steps for your people.

**Session Highlights:** People need to see our "human side," while we tend to want to hide; it will probably always take effort to overcome this; disclosure happens over time with select individuals; we must be bold, and yet careful, as we move forward to greater personal openness.

## When Community Breaks Down

**Primary Focus:** To firmly grasp the normalcy of conflict, and know the biblical steps to proceed through it.

1. Steps for conflict resolution are mentioned in the reading and Bible study question 1: acknowledge it, take initiative, no third parties, go in private, use direct communication. Which of these come easiest for you? Which are hardest? Explain why.

2. What would the "significant others" in your life wish you would do differently in conflict situations?

3. If you are facing a conflict currently in your life, how is it going? What are you learning about yourself in that situation?

---

NOTE: This question is a great one for you as a leader to model how to handle conflict—and the reality that doing so is difficult. If at all possible, it would be good for you to have an example from your life that shows that you are working hard to process the matter in an honorable way; yet also be vulnerable to your group members about ways the situation might not be going all that well. People need to see that we go at this in fits and starts, doing some things right, while at other times making mistakes.

---

4. *(Regarding questions 3 in the Bible study)* How would you describe "verbal discipline" to someone? What is your greatest weakness in this area?

5. *(Regarding question 5 and 6 in the Bible study)* What help did you get from the passages in Ephesians 4 and 1 Corinthians 13 dealing with relational breakdowns? What was your reaction to the note about being angry without sinning?

6. *(Regarding question 8 in the Bible study)* Why do we need to be concerned with what people outside the faith think about

Christians and our conflicts? Can we take this principle of modifying our behavior because of what non-Christians may think too far? Explain.

7. *(Regarding question 9 from the Bible study)* What lessons from this study do you think apply to a situation you are now facing (or apply to one in the recent past)? What can the rest of the group do to help you in your growth to live as if Jesus were in your place in this area?

**Session Highlights:** God has given us very specific instructions about handling conflict that make sense and lead to a better way to live; avoiding conflict or handling it in nonbiblical ways only leads to more problems. A little care goes a long way when it comes to our approach and choice of words in conflict situations.

---

NOTE: Remember the retreat mentioned as an option for Session 7? Don't forget to discuss it with everyone in the group. It's not too early to make plans. Also, in the next session, the spiritual exercise follows the Bible study and requires setting aside time for reflection. Encourage your members to allow enough time to thoughtfully engage in it.

---

**A Word about Leadership:** Remember the comments at the beginning of this discussion guide about your role as a leader? About now, it's probably a good idea to remind yourself that one of your key functions is to be a cheerleader—someone who seeks out signs of spiritual progress in others and makes some noise about it.

What have you seen God doing in your group members' lives as a result of this study? Don't assume that they've seen that progress—and definitely don't assume they are beyond needing simple words of encouragement. Find ways to point out to people the growth you've seen. Let them know it's happening, and that it's noticeable to you and others.

There aren't a whole lot of places in this world where people's spiritual progress is going to be recognized and celebrated. After all, wouldn't you like to hear someone cheer *you* on? So would your group members. You have the power to make a profound impact through a sincere, insightful remark.

Be aware, also, that some groups get sidetracked by a difficult member or situation that hasn't been confronted. And some individuals *could* be making significant progress—they just need a nudge. Encouragement is not about just saying nice things; it's about offering *words that urge*. It's about giving courage (en-*courage*-ment) to those who lack it.

So, take a risk. Say what needs to be said to encourage your members toward their goal of becoming fully devoted followers.

## Forgiveness

**Primary Focus:** To learn what happens—even in ourselves—when we forgive someone and take steps to actually do it.

> NOTE: As you discuss the topic of forgiveness, you may discover someone in your group has experienced deep and sustained trauma, such as childhood sexual abuse or a domestic violence situation. Some believers try to help these folks by urging them to forgive their perpetrators. While this counsel may be technically right, it is often tactically a mistake. The place to begin with such people is found in Paul's words that encourage us to "weep with those who weep" (Rom. 12:15 NRSV). The process of healing from such abuse is slow, and what most people need is just to be heard and validated. The forgiveness will come in time. Use this as a laboratory for others in the group to learn how to patiently support someone through such a process without rushing them to premature forgiveness.

1. What is your reaction to the three steps of forgiveness mentioned in the reading (rediscover the person's humanity, surrender the right to get even, wish the person well)? Recount a time, if you can, when you experienced all three as you forgave someone.

2. On the "forgive too soon" or "forgive too slow" scale, toward which side do you tend to lean? Why do you think that is true of you?

3. *(Regarding question 3 in the Bible study)* Describe a time when you withheld forgiveness. What did you believe you would gain?

4. *(Regarding the note after question 4 in the Bible study)* Put into your own words the difference between forgiveness and reconciliation. Do you agree that forgiveness is always possible but reconciliation might not be? Why?

5. *(Regarding questions 5 and 6 in the Bible study)* Why do you think people who have been forgiven so much by God still have trouble forgiving each other?

6. What truth—either directly from the Bible or from your life experience—has helped you be more forgiving? What experience has made it harder for you to be a forgiving person?

7. *(Regarding question 9 in the Bible study)* What is your reaction to the practice of "creative hypocrisy" in this area? When would it be a farce?

**Session Highlights:** Forgiveness blesses both the giver and receiver; forgiveness can be given too soon or too late; forgiveness and reconciliation are different; being completely forgiven by God forms the basis of the power and necessity to forgive others.

## Building a Passionately Inclusive Church

**Primary Focus:** To recognize our heart blockage toward certain people, and to increase love and enlarge our capacity to include.

1. Do you feel like this topic has much relevance to your life and the way you treat people? Explain.

NOTE: Fearlessly model your struggles in this area. It will help group members do the same.

2. What was your experience with the spiritual exercise this week? Did you notice a certain type of person you avoided? If you made the effort to move toward someone, what factors helped you take that risk?

3. *(Regarding question 2 in the Bible study)* Describe how growing up, your family may have had a list of those to avoid or exclude. What effect did their attitudes have on you personally?

4. *(Regarding questions 3 and 4 in the Bible study)* What blessings in your life have come to you because of God's radical desire to make a place for you? How does God's inclusion of you make a difference in the way you treat others?

5. *(Regarding question 5 in the Bible study)* Peter's exclusivity had an ironic twist: he thought he was being more spiritual by avoiding such people. Do you ever feel a twinge of righteousness in excluding certain people? In what way can spiritual status have a dividing rather than including effect?

NOTE: Sometimes we in the body of Christ become judgmental toward those outside. That can happen for a number of reasons: we find interaction with nonbelievers—and their lifestyles—offensive; they remind us of where we would be and we don't like facing that; we have a sort of pride in our spiritual accomplishments, etc. Whatever the cause, nothing could be farther from the heart of God than people who, in the name of Jesus, make some people feel as if they are "less than." The religious principles Peter was supposedly following were completely misunderstood, because God never intended his people to become smug and aloof. Help your group members face any of the potential effects of spiritual arrogance or judgmentalism and take steps to get beyond it.

6. *(Regarding question 6 in the Bible study)* What is it that keeps you from being more passionately inclusive?

7. *(Regarding question 8 in the Bible study)* Why did you rate yourself where you did on the inclusivity scale?

8. Share any of the prayers you wrote from the last question in the study.

NOTE: One way to enhance your group members' "inclusivity quotient" is by moving out of your comfort zone together. Here are three practical suggestions for investing yourselves as a group in unfamiliar experiences that stretch you and benefit others.

• *Emphasize the value of the open chair.* Consider introducing the practice of having a chair in the room that no one sits in to symbolize the many people who are still out there, unconnected to any group life. If your group is in a season of being open, when was the last time someone was invited? If your group needs to be closed for now, how can you use the open chair to make visible the value of reaching out to people?

• *Host a Seeker Party.* One great way to reach out to unsaved friends and neighbors is through a Seeker Party—a social event where you invite seekers and, in a relaxed and non-threatening way, present some facet of spiritual truth. Why not get your group members to plan such a party and invite people you know? You could pick a theme of common interest, such as parenting or marriage concerns, or host an event around a holiday (like Christmas) and make a spiritual tie-in. Is this the time for you and your group members to take a risk and step out for the sake of those who don't yet know Christ?

• *Schedule a group service project.* Planning a time for all of your group members to attend a day to help the needy not only gets people out of their comfortable surroundings, but it also has a great bonding effect on the group members. And don't forget the people you serve get blessed! Find a time when everyone can work together to serve a need of someone outside of your usual relational spheres. You may know of a family in need, or you can contact your church or a local ministry to get ideas for potential opportunities.

An important part of building a passionately inclusive church is to build a passionately inclusive small group. Find a way to help your group members experience this value in action soon.

**Session Highlights:** We need to face and get beyond our list of excluded people; such exclusivity probably goes deep and will not yield easily to attempts to change it; we were once outside, but God was gracious to us—it is unconscionable that we would not be gracious to those still outside.

NOTE: This is a last reminder about the optional retreat for the last session. If choosing this option, have all the plans been set and communicated to the group? Also, group members should complete their session in advance as normal. The retreat time will replace your usual discussion time.

## Being "For" One Another

**Primary Focus:** Just as God is powerfully for us, we are to be for the people in our relational world.

---

NOTE: The centerpiece of this group time is the opportunity for each member to express his or her words of encouragement to each of the other members of the group. (One thing I really appreciate about you is . . .) Needless to say, this experience will lose its meaning if it is rushed. Time could be a particular problem, especially for groups with limited discussion time. Here are a few options:

- If at all possible, do this final discussion as a retreat (see the following retreat guide). That way, the session material can be processed slowly over the course of an overnight retreat with the encouragement exercise as the final experience. If you choose this option, skip the questions below and go directly to the retreat guide. All of the discussion questions have been included in the retreat guide (although structured somewhat differently), so you won't need to refer back to this sheet.
- If this is not possible, consider doing the session over two group meetings.
- If neither of the above is an option, pick one or two of the discussion questions below, and then move directly to the encouragement exercise, allowing as much time as possible for it.

---

1. *(Regarding question 1 in the Bible study)* Who was the person who was *for* you? How did they tangibly express that? What impact did it have on you?

2. *(Regarding questions 2–4 in the Bible study)* How easy is it for you these days to feel that God is *for* you? What part of your study of Romans 8 had the most impact for you?

3. *(Regarding question 3 in the Bible study)* What tempts you to feel distant or separated from God these days? Where do you most need a spirit of "truly reverent defiance"?

4. How did the spiritual exercise go? When was it easy for you to be *for* someone? When was it a real stretch? What do you perceive made the difference? Did people's responses surprise you in any way?

5. *(Regarding question 7 in the Bible study)* Describe a time when someone's encouragement took the form of tough or challenging words. How did you respond initially? What ways did growth happen specifically because of that experience?

6. How did you react to the statement from the reading, ". . . that was not the last time I've turned church into a contest"? How often do competition, comparisons, or envy keep you from being wholeheartedly *for* others—even in the church?

7. Where do you need encouragement in this season of your life?

**Encouragement Exercise:** Now it is time to stop talking about encouragement and to actually do it. Put numbers in a hat and have each person pick a number to determine the order. The person with number 1 goes first. Have that person sit in a chair which is facing everyone else in the group. Then, everyone else should pull out their encouragement statements about that person and either read or paraphrase them. The person being "appreciated" should not comment on the statements other than to say thank-you. There is one exception to this rule. The person being encouraged may ask the encourager, "What do you mean by that?" or a similar question for clarification. Continue in the order of the numbers people picked until everyone has been in the "encouragement seat."

Finally, end with a prayer time. Be sure to emphasize gratitude for how this exercise tangibly models how God is *for* us and how he wants to encourage us. It also shows the wonder of the body of Christ, and how we can bring meaningful gifts to each other through something as simple as encouraging words. Also, pray for the requests people made earlier about areas in which they need encouragement.

# RETREAT GUIDE

## Being "For" One Another

**Primary Focus:** To deepen your experience with God and your small group through giving and receiving encouragement.

This retreat is designed as an overnight getaway—Friday supper to Saturday late afternoon, for example. You will find that such concentrated time together as a group enables you, in one twenty-four-hour period, to do a remarkable amount of growing. This event can pay rich dividends for your personal spiritual growth and significantly enhance your group experience—both now and in the months to come.

### Retreat Overview

Part One (Evening)—Icebreaker and discussion

Part Two (Next morning and early afternoon)—Solitude (and debrief)

Part Three (Late afternoon)—Encouragement exercise

The retreat has three main parts or stages. As the leader, feel free to structure the various elements of the experience to fit the needs of your group members. (Of course, if you have ideas beyond our suggestions that enhance the retreat, use them as well.) The only aspect that is nonnegotiable is the encouragement exercise at the end (Part Three).

As you think about where to conduct this retreat, consider the tone set by the location. Because you will require a relatively distraction-free environment with time for quiet reflection, the facility you use ought to have quiet meeting places. If you decide to go to a hotel, for example, they'll need to have a room where you won't be interrupted, and hopefully have several quiet spaces for group members to go to during the day. On the other hand, if the facilities are too basic, people may feel uncomfortable and cooped up. Ideally, find a location that has an isolated, comfortable central meeting room for group times, grounds for walks (weather permitting), and several quiet nooks or corners without a lot of traffic.

You do not need to spend a lot of money to make your retreat work. If necessary, simply meeting at someone's house—provided there are no interruptions—could create the right atmosphere for your retreat.

Here is one possible schedule for the retreat:

### Friday—Part One

| | |
|---|---|
| 6:30–8:30 p.m. | Supper together, icebreaker, and discussion |
| 8:30–10:30 p.m. | Social activity |

### Saturday—Parts Two and Three

| | |
|---|---|
| 8–9 a.m. | Breakfast |
| 9–9:30 a.m. | Orientation to the day, prayer |
| 9:30–11:30 a.m. | Solitude |
| 12–2:30 p.m. | Extended lunch; solitude debrief and discussion |
| 2:30–3 p.m. | Break |
| 3–5:30 p.m. | Encouragement exercise |

You could also compress these stages into a single day (for example, Parts One and Two on Saturday morning and Part Three in the afternoon), though we encourage you to take the full amount of time for the experience to unfold at an unhurried pace.

Before you do this retreat, everyone in your small group needs to have read Session 7, "Being 'For' One Another," have answered the questions in the Bible study, and have completed the spiritual exercise (including the fill-in-the-blank encouragement note to each person). Be sure everyone brings a Bible, the workbook, and a journal, if desired, to provide extra writing space for the solitude exercise. Other than that, members do not need to do any specific preparation.

### Part One

(Friday evening)—Supper, Icebreaker, and Discussion

The purpose of this first part of the retreat is to have fun and enjoy being with each other, while also beginning to discuss aspects of the session. During supper together, spend some time discussing the questions below. Then, play together. (If you prefer, play first and end the night with the icebreaker and discussion—it's up to you.) The important thing to keep in mind is not to do too much at night because if people are tired, the activities of the next day won't work as well.

The essence of the icebreaker is to get to have people let down their guard a little by answering one or more of the following questions:

- If money and logistics were not a factor, how would you want to spend your ideal twenty-four-hour day?
- Tell us about one of the most foolhardy, risky, or embarrassing things you've ever done.

When you've done the icebreaker, discuss the following questions based on the session completed before the retreat:

- Describe a time in your life when someone was strongly *for* you. How did they express that? How did it impact you?
- How did the spiritual exercise go during the week? When was it easy to be *for* others? When was it a stretch? Did you notice comparison or envy keeping you from being *for* someone?

When the discussion has ended, head out to the social time you have planned. Keep in mind that whatever you decide to do, the event needs to allow for people to really be with each other and not isolated. If you were to go to a movie or concert, for example, everyone sits silent for two hours without connecting with each other. Pick an activity which allows for free-flowing conversation, or at least some kind of personal interaction. Our suggestions include:

Bowling
Miniature golf
Picnic supper or barbecue
Square dancing or swing dancing
Roller-skating
Sporting event
Game night (Charades, Pictionary, Murder Mystery, etc.)

(Remember, don't stay out too late or people will be tired the next morning.)

## Part Two

(Saturday morning and early afternoon)—Breakfast, Solitude, and Lunch Debrief

After you finish breakfast in the morning, gather everyone to explain how the rest of the day will unfold. Go over the schedule with them, and then orient them to the solitude exercise. For some, intentionally being alone and quiet may be an unfamiliar way to spend a couple of hours. Explain the value of getting away from distractions to focus on some aspect of God and his truth. Point out that paying attention to how we react in solitude is also part of what we can learn from it. The Solitude Worksheet found in Session 7 of the Bible study explains what to reflect on during the time, so people shouldn't feel too threatened that they won't know what to do as they head off on their own.

Explain that everyone needs to find a place where they won't be interrupted until lunch. They should use the Solitude Worksheet as a guide. Have them also bring the statements of appreciation they wrote out for each person in preparation for the meeting. (Note: If they haven't done this yet, this time will give them a way to complete this assignment so everyone will be prepared for the last segment of the retreat.) Encourage them to make notes as they go through the Solitude Worksheet. End this time with some prayer, inviting God to work in the group members collectively through the retreat, and also specifically in the solitude time that follows. Be sure to indicate at what time they will regroup before you dismiss them.

When the solitude experience is over, meet together for lunch. Be sure everyone has their discussion guides with the completed Solitude Worksheet. We suggest you begin this discussion during the meal and continue the conversation after the meal is over. If at all possible, set it up so you don't have to move anywhere as the conversation continues.

While everyone is eating, begin the discussion with questions such as:

How did the solitude time go for you?
What was a highlight from your time alone?
What did you notice about the drift of your mind as you got quiet?

As the conversation moves on, ask the group members:

How easy was it for you to feel God encouraging you?

People will have a variety of answers. For some, the experience of solitude opens them up to the Spirit's work; for others, alone time leaves them feeling bored or confused. Some hear God clearly; others feel as if God never talks to them, or they analyze impressions received and can't seem to discern what's from God and what's their own thinking. Also, if some have a more negative temperament, receiving encouragement will always be hard, regardless of where it's from—God or other people.

Finally, ask everyone to answer the question:

Where do you need encouragement in this season of your life?

Some people may become emotional as they share struggles or heartbreaks. Follow Paul's advice and "weep with those who weep" (Rom. 12:15 NRSV). Be sure that you take notes on what everyone says so you can be an encourager in those areas. A follow-up card over the next few weeks to each group member with specific words of encouragement would be a great blessing.

When you have finished discussing these questions, be sure to take a break. Allow group members to stretch, use the restroom, get a drink, etc. We recommend at least a half-hour break before heading into the home stretch.

## Part Three

(Late afternoon)—Encouragement Exercise

This final part is the climax of the retreat. Be sure to allocate sufficient time for everyone to get their turn—probably around fifteen to twenty minutes for each person in your group. It is imperative that no interruptions occur during this time—be sure you've picked a completely distraction-free environment.

Put numbers in a hat and have each person pick a number to determine the order. The person with number 1 goes first. Have that person sit in a chair facing everyone else in the group. Then, everyone else should pull out their encouragement statements about that person and either read or paraphrase them. The person being "appreciated" should not comment on the statements other than to say "thank you." There is one exception to this rule: The person being encouraged may ask the encourager, "What do you mean by that?" or a similar question for clarification. Continue in order of the numbers people picked until everyone has been in the "encouragement seat."

Finally, end your retreat with a prayer time. Be sure to emphasize gratitude for how this exercise tangibly models how God is *for* us, and how he wants to encourage us. It also shows the wonder of the body of Christ, and how we can bring meaningful gifts to each other through something as simple as encouraging words. Also pray for the requests people made earlier about areas in which they need encouragement.

**John C. Ortberg Jr.** is teaching pastor at Willow Creek Community Church in South Barrington, Illinois. He is the author of *The Life You've Always Wanted* and *Love Beyond Reason*. John and his wife, Nancy, live in the Chicago area with their three children, Laura, Mallory, and Johnny.

**Laurie Pederson**, a real estate investment manager, is a founding member of Willow Creek Community Church. As an elder since 1978, she has helped shape many of the foundational values and guiding principles of the church. She is cocreator of Willow Creek's discipleship-based church membership process. Laurie lives outside of Chicago with her husband, Scott.

**Judson Poling**, a staff member at Willow Creek Community Church since 1980, writes small group training materials and many of the dramas performed in Willow Creek's outreach services. He is coauthor of the *Walking with God* and *Tough Questions* Bible study series and general editor of *The Journey: A Study Bible for Spiritual Seekers*. He lives in Algonquin, Illinois, with his wife, Deb, and their two children, Anna and Ryan.

# Willow Creek Association
*Vision, Training, Resources for Prevailing Churches*

This resource was created to serve you and to help you in building a local church that prevails!

Since 1992, the Willow Creek Association (WCA) has been linking like-minded, action-oriented churches with each other and with strategic vision, training, and resources. Now a worldwide network of over 6,400 churches from more than ninety denominations, the WCA works to equip Member Churches and others with the tools needed to build prevailing churches. Our desire is to inspire, equip, and encourage Christian leaders to build biblically functioning churches that reach increasing numbers of unchurched people, not just with innovations from Willow Creek Community Church in South Barrington, Illinois, but from any church in the world that has experienced God-given breakthroughs.

## WILLOW CREEK CONFERENCES

Each year, thousands of local church leaders, staff and volunteers—from WCA Member Churches and others—attend one of our conferences or training events. Conferences offered on the Willow Creek campus in South Barrington, Illinois, include:

**Prevailing Church Conference:** Foundational training for staff and volunteers working to build a prevailing local church.

**Prevailing Church Workshops:** More than fifty strategic, day-long workshops covering seven topic areas that represent key characteristics of a prevailing church; offered twice each year.

**Promiseland Conference:** Children's ministries; infant through fifth grade.

**Student Ministries Conference:** Junior and senior high ministries.

**Willow Creek Arts Conference:** Vision and training for Christian artists using their gifts in the ministries of local churches.

**Leadership Summit:** Envisioning and equipping Christians with leadership gifts and responsibilities; broadcast live via satellite to eighteen cities across North America.

**Contagious Evangelism Conference:** Encouragement and training for churches and church leaders who want to be strategic in reaching lost people for Christ.

**Small Groups Conference:** Exploring how developing a church *of* small groups can play a vital role in developing authentic Christian community that leads to spiritual transformation.

To find out more about WCA conferences, visit our website at www.willowcreek.com.

## PREVAILING CHURCH REGIONAL WORKSHOPS

Each year the WCA team leads several, two-day training events in select cities across the United States. Some twenty day-long workshops are offered in topic areas including leadership, next-generation ministries, small groups, arts and worship, evangelism, spiritual gifts, financial stewardship, and spiritual formation. These events make quality training more accessible and affordable to larger groups of staff and volunteers.

To find out more about Prevailing Church Regional Workshops, visit our website at www.willowcreek.com.

## WILLOW CREEK RESOURCES™

Churches can look to Willow Creek Resources™ for a trusted channel of ministry tools in areas of leadership, evangelism, spiritual gifts, small groups, drama, contemporary music, financial stewardship, spiritual transformation, and more. For ordering information, call (800) 570-9812 or visit our website at www.willowcreek.com.

## WCA MEMBERSHIP

Membership in the Willow Creek Association as well as attendance at WCA Conferences is for churches, ministries, and leaders who hold to a historic, orthodox understanding of biblical Christianity. The annual church membership fee of $249 provides substantial discounts for your entire team on all conferences and Willow Creek Resources, networking opportunities with other outreach-oriented churches, a bimonthly newsletter, a subscription to the *Defining Moments* monthly audio journal for leaders, and more.

To find out more about WCA membership, visit our website at www.willowcreek.com.

## WILLOWNET (WWW.WILLOWCREEK.COM)

This Internet resource service provides access to hundreds of Willow Creek messages, drama scripts, songs, videos, and multimedia ideas. The system allows you to sort through these elements and download them for a fee.

Our website also provides detailed information on the Willow Creek Association, Willow Creek Community Church, WCA membership, conferences, training events, resources, and more.

## WILLOWCHARTS.COM (WWW.WILLOWCHARTS.COM)

Designed for local church worship leaders and musicians, WillowCharts.com provides online access to hundreds of music charts and chart components, including choir, orchestral, and horn sections, as well as rehearsal tracks and video streaming of Willow Creek Community Church performances.

## THE NET (HTTP://STUDENTMINISTRY.WILLOWCREEK.COM)

The NET is an online training and resource center designed by and for student ministry leaders. It provides an inside look at the structure, vision, and mission of prevailing student ministries from around the world. The NET gives leaders access to complete programming elements, including message outlines, dramas, small group questions, and more. An indispensable resource and networking tool for prevailing student ministry leaders!

## CONTACT THE WILLOW CREEK ASSOCIATION

If you have comments or questions, or would like to find out more about WCA events or resources, please contact us:

### Willow Creek Association
P.O. Box 3188, Barrington, IL 60011-3188
Phone: (800) 570-9812 or (847) 765-0070
Fax (888) 922-0035 or (847) 765-5046
Web: www.willowcreek.com

a place where ...

# nobody stands alone!

Small groups, when they're working right, provide a place where you can experience continuous growth and community—the deepest level of community, modeled after the church in Acts 2, where believers are devoted to Christ's teachings and to fellowship with each other.

If you'd like to take the next step in building that kind of small group environment for yourself or for your church, we'd like to help.

The Willow Creek Association in South Barrington, Illinois, hosts an annual Small Groups Conference attended by thousands of church and small group leaders from around the world. Each year we also lead small group training events and workshops in seven additional cities across the country. We offer a number of small group resources for both small groups and small group leaders available to you through your local bookstore and Willow Creek Resources.

If you'd like to learn more, contact the Willow Creek Association at 1-800-570-9812. Or visit us on-line: www.willowcreek.com.

# continue the transformation . . .

## PURSUING SPIRITUAL TRANSFORMATION

JOHN ORTBERG, LAURIE PEDERSON, JUDSON POLING

Experience a radical change in how you think and how you live. Forget about trying hard to be a better person. Welcome instead to the richly rewarding process of discovering and growing into the person God made you to be! Developed by Willow Creek Community Church as its core curriculum, this planned, progressive small group approach to spiritual maturity will help you:

- Become more like Jesus
- Recapture the image of God in your life
- Cultivate intimacy with God
- Live your faith everywhere, all the time
- Renew your zest for life

*Leader's guide included!*

*Fully Devoted:*
*Living Each Day in Jesus' Name*          0-310-22073-4

*Grace:*
*An Invitation to a Way of Life*          0-310-22074-2

*Growth:*
*Training vs. Trying*          0-310-22075-0

*Groups:*
*The Life-Giving Power of Community*          0-310-22076-9

*Gifts:*
*The Joy of Serving God*          0-310-22077-7

*Giving:*
*Unlocking the Heart of Good Stewardship*          0-310-22078-5

*Look for* Pursuing Spiritual Transformation *at your local bookstore.*

**WILLOW CREEK**
RESOURCES          www.willowcreek.com

**ZONDERVAN**™

GRAND RAPIDS, MICHIGAN 49530
www.zondervan.com

# If You Want to Walk on Water, You've Got to Get Out of the Boat

## JOHN ORTBERG

*It's one thing to try to walk on water and sink sometimes. But the real failure is to never get out of the boat.*

**We were made for something more than avoiding failure.** As followers of Jesus, we want to go where he calls us. We want to step out in faith. But walk on water? What does that mean?

Walking on water means facing your fears and choosing not to let fear have the last word.
Walking on water means discovering and embracing the unique calling of God on your life.
Walking on water means experiencing the power of God in your life to do something you would not be capable of doing on your own.

JOHN ORTBERG
*author of* THE LIFE YOU'VE ALWAYS WANTED

IF YOU WANT TO WALK ON WATER, YOU'VE GOT TO GET OUT OF THE BOAT

**Hardcover 0-310-22863-8**

John Ortberg, in his engaging and humorous style, reflects on this story in Matthew 14. He helps us recognize what boat we're in—the comfortable situation where we're hiding. He reminds us that there is a storm outside the boat—we will encounter problems. But if we're willing to get out of the boat, two things will happen. First, when we fail—and we will fail sometimes—Jesus will be there to pick us up. We will not fail alone. We will find he is wholly adequate to save us. And the second thing is, every once in a while, we'll walk on water! Because "if you want to walk on water, you've got to get out of the boat."

**ZONDERVAN**™

GRAND RAPIDS, MICHIGAN 49530

w w w . z o n d e r v a n . c o m

# Transform Your Church and Small Groups

## Community 101
### Gilbert Bilezikian

Written by one of Willow Creek's founders, this resource will help your church become a true community of believers. Bilezikian uses the Bible as his guide to demonstrate the centrality of community in God's plan of salvation and describe how it can be expressed in the daily life of the church.

Softcover – ISBN: 0-310-21741-5

## Leading Life-Changing Small Groups
### Bill Donahue and the Willow Creek Small Groups Team

Get the comprehensive guidance you need to cultivate life-changing small groups and growing, fruitful believers. Willow Creek's director of adult education and training shares in-depth the practical insights that have made Willow Creek's small group ministry so incredibly effective.

Softcover – ISBN: 0-310-20595-6

## Available at your local bookstore!